ROSE
COLORED
GLASSES

UPLIFTING LIFE STRATEGIES
FOR TEENS

REBBETZIN S. FELDBRAND

ISRAEL BOOKSHOP
Publications

REBBETZIN S. FELDBRAND

ROSE
COLORED
GLASSES

UPLIFTING LIFE STRATEGIES
FOR TEENS

I would like to express my thanks to Tova Younger, editor;
Rivkah Lewis, cover and book design.

Printed in the USA

Distributed by:
Israel Bookshop Publications
501 Prospect Street
Lakewood, NJ 08701

Tel: (732) 901-3009
Fax: (732) 901-4012
www.israelbookshoppublications.com
info@israelbookshoppublications.com

Rabbi Zev Leff

Rabbi of Moshav Matityahu
Rosh HaYeshiva—Yeshiva Gedola Matityahu

הרב זאב לף

מרא דאתרא מושב מתתיהו
ראש הישיבה—ישיבה גדולה מתתיהו

D.N. Modiin 71917   Tel: 08—976—1138 טל'   Fax: 08—976—5326 פקס'   ד.נ. מודיעין 71917

Dear Friends,

I have read portions of the manuscript *Rose-Colored Glasses; Uplifting Life Strategies for Teens* by Rebbetzin S. Feldbrand. Although it is a long time since I was a teenager, I found the work interesting, uplifting, enlightening and inspiring.

The authoress presents many and varied Torah sources to give one the means to acquire a healthy positive view of themselves and of life in general. The presentation is spiced with relevant anecdotes, sound practical advice and food for thought.

This manual for personal growth and development is a valuable contribution to the Torah community. I recommend that parents give this as a gift to their teenage children and then borrow the book for their own edification.

I commend the authoress on the presentation that is a true kiddush Hashem in both its form and substance.

I pray that Hashem bless her and her family with life, health and the wherewithal to benefit the community with further works.

Sincerely with Torah blessings,

Zev Leff

Table of Contents

INTRODUCTION

Here is the manual you have been waiting for! Have you been wondering how to manage your life better? Maximize your opportunities? Or maybe even pondering what exactly you are doing here?

Hashem placed you on this planet and gifted you with a body, endowing it with character and middos. He created a wondrous world to assist you and told you to get busy completing your assignment; the assignment specified by the words *His'halech lefanai ve'hayai samim*– "Walk before me and become perfect" (Bereishis 17:1). Let's take a moment to think about this idea. Hashem's glorious world, as well as your individually selected custom-designed personal resources, are the tools needed to successfully complete The Mission.

Begin by looking outward. How uplifted you become

when you realize how many forces were created to serve each person – including you! Every blade of grass is controlled by an angel that causes it to grow (Bereishis Rabba 10:6-7). You may casually walk on thousands of blades of grass, not considering the great wisdom and unequalled loyalty of the thousands of *malachim* who are there for you.

Your heart should fill with the wonder of this glorious potential and gratitude for this magnificent gift. Everything in the entire world - from its most general laws to its finest details - serves as lamps lighting your way towards an understanding of *bechol derachecha da'eihu*– "In all your paths you shall know Him" (Alter of Slobodka).

Now turn your eyes inward. No human being was created for mediocrity. Hashem gave us strengths, abilities and talents so that we can set our sights high and reach for the stars. True, we have limitations but we also have tremendous strengths. The first step in undertaking our Mission is to break away from any and all limiting beliefs, both ours and others.

> *In India, elephants are still being trained to perform difficult physical labor. The elephant trainer will pull the elephant by a rope from one demanding task to another. At night when the elephant's heavy labor is over, the trainer ties the elephant's rope to a peg in the ground.*
>
> *Anyone who witnesses this process would surely question the elephant's submissiveness. The rope is not significant and neither is the peg. A behemoth of that size could easily ignore his trainer with his rope and peg and walk off into the forest.*
>
> *There is a reason that the elephant makes no effort to break away. When the elephant is born he weighs*

about two hundred and fifty pounds. From day one he is tied to the peg in the ground. He tries to escape but he can't. He keeps trying again and again but escape is impossible. He tries for a week and for a month. After all those attempts the elephant learns the lesson: the rope is too strong and the peg is too deep. That lesson remains fixed in his mind for the rest of his life, even after he has attained full maturity and weighs fourteen thousand pounds. He remains compliant because in his limited understanding he can't escape.

That's an apt parable for many people who don't become a fraction of what they could. Not because they don't have talents or abilities, but because they have limiting beliefs. They are like the mighty elephant that is kept in check by his belief in the strength of a rope which is not really strong enough.

It doesn't matter how great you could be if you think you can't. If you consider yourself to be a simple, ordinary person, then you will live up to exactly that which you believe, and no more. You have numerous gifts! Make up your mind to use them – use them for Hashem's sake. Resolve to take your aspirations to the highest level (Heard from Rabbi B.Z. Shafier).

It has been said, "Whether you think you can, or think you can't, you are right!"

Rav Ovadia Yosef would often recount that Napoleon would gather young troops and say, "Is there anyone in this group who does not dream of being a general one day? If there's even one of you who doesn't harbor such aspirations, please leave. If you want to accomplish anything, you must dream of reaching the top" (Maran Harav Ovadia, page 435).

The same applies to you, dear reader. If you don't dream of becoming a great person, you will never be able to achieve much success.

Food For Thought

We all know that when *Moshe Rabbeinu* was an infant he refused to nurse from any of Basya's nursemaids, because it was only proper that the mouth that would eventually speak with Hashem should receive milk only from a kosher source.

What is interesting is that the Rema on Yoreh De'ah 81:7 derives from here that a Jewish baby should preferably not nurse from a gentile woman.

It is easy to understand why Moshe *Rabbeinu* wouldn't be permitted to nurse from a gentile woman because he would later receive the gift of prophecy. But how does that apply to other children? The majority of Jewish children will never receive prophecy. Why then shouldn't they nurse from a gentile?

Rav Yaakov Kaminetzky explains that each person has the potential to become great enough to speak with the *Shechinah*. We must therefore not do anything which might prevent us from reaching the loftiest spiritual levels possible.

The concepts I have included in this book are meant to assist you to climb higher and higher throughout your life. They will allow you to highlight your ability to add to this world in your own special way. You will be absolutely amazed at the incredible amount of power inside of you. Reading this work will help you select goals and set you on the path to success.

You will walk decisively and steadily towards happiness and fulfillment. The journey to the best of who you are is full of excitement and so rewarding. As you read, highlight/underline those sections that "talk" to you so that you can easily find these passages when needed, to help you get the most out of new situations in life. A story too, can provide the insight that will load your fuel tanks, and allow you to take full advantage of opportunities that come your way.

There might be times in your life when you find yourself in a disheartening place and you will need to summon up all the assistance Hashem has laid out for you. The tools in this book will help you improve your ability to handle any situation. Refer to this encouraging resource any time you feel the need. Each time a new challenge comes into your life you need only reach for one of these concepts to move yourself from the weakest to the strongest part of who you are.

Learn to view your life as a game! Not just any simple game, but a challenging game. And thrill with each advance. Yes, life is serious, but using some gaming techniques and attitudes will lighten your journey through life – and that will put you in a constant state of *simcha*. Never forget, *Ain simcha k'simchas mitvah*–There's no *simcha* like the happiness that can be extracted from the performance of a mitzvah!

May you merit seeing Hashem guiding you towards success in all your endeavors.

DAVEN

EFFECTS OF *TEFILLAH*

The effects of *tefillah* are unbelievable. Deep down, inside each of us, lies a great treasure of purity and light which is released when we *daven* with *kavanah*. *Tefillah* can make us great if we work on it properly, but we have to follow up with action that demonstrates that we really mean what we are saying. With repeated *tefillah* and appropriate follow up you can become a different person, rising to a level of joyous connection to Hashem.

PRAY LIKE A CHILD

Rav Moshe Midner *zy"a* would say that one should pray like a son pleading with his father. When a child begs for something, he isn't shy about expressing himself. If you aren't opening up fully as you *daven*, it indicates that you don't view yourself as a child of Hashem.

HASHEM PLACES HIS EAR NEXT TO YOUR MOUTH

When you *daven*, Hashem places His ear next to your mouth (*Yerushalmi*). People think that *tefillah* brings us closer to Hashem, with Hashem remaining where He is in heaven. But in truth, Hashem responds to our level of devotion and correspondingly comes down to us to listen to our *tefillos* (Based on the *Maharal*'s discussion of the *keruvim*). There is a direct correlation between the power of our cries to Him and His closeness to us (*Sefas Emes, Va'eschanan*).

DAVENING IS A GIFT FROM HASHEM

There is nothing like *davening* to construct the wings you need to soar. *Davening* is a gift from Hashem to enable us to connect to him in times of sorrow or with thanksgiving in a time of happiness. In addition, we benefit by having our *tefillos* answered.

"TEFILLAH MEANS 'TO THINK.' LE'HISPALLEL MEANS 'TO MAKE YOURSELF THINK.' WE HAVE TO THINK OF HASHEM AND THEN HE'LL THINK OF US"

(RABBI AVIDGDOR MILLER).

DAVENING GETS US EVERYTHING WE NEED

A person's money, wisdom and strength cannot compete with the effectiveness of his *tefillos* (Shochar Tov). Using *tefillah*, a person has the ability to attain everything that is good (Chazon Ish). Cries of the mouth are not nearly as effective as cries of the heart (Rav Yechezkel Levenstein). *Davening* from the bottom of the heart can shatter iron barriers which prevent salvation from reaching us.

> *A fierce bear attacked a man in the forest. Frightened, he grabbed a stick and began hitting the animal. To his delight, the bear fell to the ground; the man gratefully kissed his stick.*
>
> *As he turned to leave, he saw a man who laughingly told him, "Do you think your stick killed the bear? I was hiding in a tree, and I shot the bear dead with my gun!"*

The Ben Ish Chai explains that people think that their efforts enable them to achieve their goals, but really it's their *tefillos* that do it (Ben Ish Chai).

"ONE MUST BE CONFIDENT THAT ONE'S TEFILLAH SPLITS THE FIRMAMENTS AND RISES TO HASHEM"

(TIFERES SHLOMO).

HOW TO DAVEN WELL

How can you achieve heartfelt *kavanah*? Take a few moments to prepare for *davening*. This will raise your *tefillos* to greater heights. Another way is to talk to Hashem often.

"One should accustom oneself to *daven* for everything; for the minor things and for the important issues in life. When one becomes accustomed to this practice, he will always be connected to Hashem" (Rebbe Reb Bunim). When a connected person begins praying he is automatically starting at a higher level.

"AS THE FLAME CLOTHES A BLACK SOOTY LUMP OF COAL IN A GARMENT OF FIRE AND RELEASES THE HEAT IMPRISONED THEREIN, SO DOES TEFILLAH CLOTHE A PERSON IN A GARMENT OF HOLINESS, FREEING THE LIGHT AND FIRE IMPLANTED WITHIN US BY OUR MAKER. THIS LIGHT THEN ILLUMINATES HIS WHOLE BEING" (ZOHAR).

EVEN THE WORST OF *TEFILLOS* IS REMARKABLE

To heighten your feelings of devotion, set aside time to learn the meaning of the words you are saying. Even if you believe that your *tefillos* are as worthless as a zero continue praying. Your recorded zeros will become a large number on the day that you *daven* with great *kavanah*, for on that day Hashem will add a one to your zeros. Each *tefillah* (even the prayer said when our mind was elsewhere) is good, for it serves as the basis for our *tefillos* uttered with heartfelt devotion (Tchortkover Rebbe).

EXPECT HASHEM TO ANSWER YOUR *TEFILLOS*

When we *daven* we should expect Hashem to answer our *tefillos*. We are the children of the Creator of the Universe. As a result we can be certain that the Creator will come through for us. Imagine you have a rich father. Would he refuse to help you when you need something? Not likely. He will surely say, "Look, she is depending on me. She has nowhere else to turn."

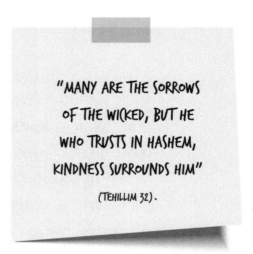

"MANY ARE THE SORROWS OF THE WICKED, BUT HE WHO TRUSTS IN HASHEM, KINDNESS SURROUNDS HIM" (TEHILLIM 32).

NEVER BECOME DISCOURAGED

We should never become discouraged, even if it appears that our *tefillos* are being ignored. Allow your *tefillos* to soothe your soul and just keep praying. It is possible that we are missing just one more *tefillah* to make up the total that will get us what we need. Because it is so easy to lose heart, the *possuk* encourages us to remain hopeful and enthusiastic. "Trust in Hashem, strengthen your hearts and trust in Hashem" (*Tehillim* 27).

SUBMERGE OVERFLOWING EMOTIONS IN *TEFILLAH*

Bottom line, we will benefit greatly by placing ourselves in Hashem's hands. The natural product of that trust is a special closeness, which enables us to interact with Hashem without any obstacles holding back His miracles. Tip! - When your emotions overflow, submerge them in the words of *tefillah*.

> *Little Boruch Ber's behavior needed some correction. When his father stopped shouting the child turned to leave the room. "Where are you going?" his father asked.*
>
> *"If I am crying anyway I am going to say* Tehillim," *the child replied.*

Before starting any project large or small, turn to Hashem in *tefillah*. Don't forget!

> *The Baal Shem Tov sent one of his talmidim to supervise the production of wine for the Rebbe and the chassidim. The assignment required that he make sure that a non-Jew did not touch the finished product. On the way back home the barrel sat at his side so that he could keep his eyes on it. At one point the wagon lurched throwing the student to one side and the barrel to the other. The non-Jewish driver took hold of the barrel to prevent it from falling. The student was devastated. After so much effort and so close to home, the wine had become unkosher.*
>
> *The Baal Shem Tov nodded sadly when he saw his talmid. "You never once* davened *for the success of your mission," he explained.*

The Chafetz Chaim's daughter once related the following story concerning her grandmother:

> *My grandmother was not a miracle worker. I do remember that at the end of her life, after her son, my father, had become renown throughout the Torah world*

as the saintly Chafetz Chaim, a number of close friends approached her with the obvious question: "How did you merit having a son who illuminates the eyes of the world? What was your recipe for success?"

She replied that she could not remember having done anything special.

They did not give up so easily, however. After they asked her again and again, my grandmother did admit that there was one small thing that came to mind. "Before my wedding, my mother spoke to me. These were her words: 'My daughter, listen to what I have to say. We are commanded to raise our sons to study Torah and fear of Heaven. Therefore, I ask of you that every free moment that you have, take your siddur in hand and pray to Hashem that you merit to raise your children to be G-d-fearing and observant Jews who will devote themselves to Torah study. Do not forget to shed tears when you pray.' She then gave me a siddur which included Sefer Tehillim. That's all I did. Whenever I had a free moment, I would take out the siddur and recite Tehillim, crying out my heart to Hashem, begging Him to help my Yisrael'ke develop into a Torah scholar, and a yarei Shamayim."

When relating this story, Rav Eliezer M. Shach would add, "Rashi's rebbe was Rabbeinu Gershom Me'or Ha'goleh. He was greater than Rashi. Yet, Rashi merited becoming the Rabbon Shel Kol Yisrael, quintessential Torah teacher of the Jewish people. Why? Because of his mother, the tzadekes, who was the sister of Rabbeinu Shimon Hazekein from Magenza and because of his saintly father, and their continuous tefillos on his behalf."

It's never too early to *daven* for something important.

Reb Tevye's daughter Chana had been in shidduchim *for three years. From the time she entered the
parsha, Chana davened each day to meet her zivug,
asking Hashem to send her a husband who is a Torah
scholar and with whom she can build a home filled with
Torah and fear of Hashem. Things did not go quickly but
Chana tried her best to maintain a positive disposition,
reminding herself that shidduchim like everything else
in this world, are orchestrated by Hashem.*

One day a shidduch was suggested which sounded
like someone special. He was a ben Torah who was among
the elite students of his yeshivah. In short order, a "yes"
was given and Dovid and Chana met; shortly thereafter,
they were engaged. Their wedding was a truly joyous
occasion for both sides, but especially for Chana, who
had waited so long for this special day.

One night after their marriage, Chana stood giving
thanks for her husband's sterling middos and his un-
concealed love of Torah. She shared with him how much
she had davened for a husband of this caliber. "Baruch
Hashem, my dream came true," she said, her eyes shining.

Dovid listened with his forehead creased. Turning
to his wife, he asked, "Do you remember precisely when
you began to daven for this?"

Chana thought for a few moments and then recalled
exactly when she was inspired to begin davening for a
husband who would be a genuine Torah scholar.

Dovid was extremely moved by what she said. He
began to cry quietly. Chana saw that they were not tears
of sadness.

"As a teen I struggled greatly with my learning. As hard as I tried, I just couldn't seem to excel. At one point however I was infused with an enthusiasm for learning. I felt a great drive to learn and began to understand everything far better. I was privileged to reach the heights that you were davening for. And remarkably, it was at the exact time that you began davening that my personal shift for the better took place."

In telling this story, Rav Gamliel Rabinovich pointed out that very often we don't know what our *tefillos* are accomplishing. For three years, Chana *davened* for an outstanding husband, but as each day passed with no obvious results she felt like her *tefillos* were accomplishing nothing. She had no idea that her *tefillos* were helping her future husband grow in Torah and spirituality. Dovid as well had no idea that the *tefillos* of his future wife were the reason that he was meriting such a great measure of help from *Shamayim*.

DO NOT BE AFRAID

PEOPLE ARE AFRAID OF MANY THINGS

People can be afraid of many things. Each new situation may be accompanied by its own set of fears. Fear can sometimes keep you from moving ahead with your life. Some worry about dealing with change. Others find beginnings difficult or ends scary. Challenges such as asserting yourself, making decisions and meeting new friends can be complicated. It can be comforting to know that these issues frighten adults as well.

THE VOICE OF FEAR IS THE VOICE OF THE YETZER HARA

You may dread the thought of being helpless, of not being liked. Possibly you worry about trying something new and failing. There might be a nonstop little voice inside that says things like, "You'll never pull it off, don't take any chances, you will make a mistake." Realize that all of these fears are the voice of the *yetzer hara*. Once identified, he can be more aggressively opposed.

It is important to remember that we are expected to use the mental and physical capacity with which we have been endowed. Hashem requires no more of you than you are capable of.

REMEMBER THE FEARS YOU HAVE OVERCOME

Whenever you find yourself doubting how far you can go, think about how far you have come. Remember everything you have faced, all the battles you have won and all the fears you have overcome.

ASK HASHEM TO HELP YOU OVERCOME YOUR FEAR

Whenever you are feeling fearful and your *yetzer hara* says "you won't be able to handle it," remember to ask Hashem for help. Say the words, "*Ribono Shel Olam* I am afraid, please help me be strong." Then tell yourself that Hashem is at your side assisting you. With help like that, you can handle anything.

EFFECTIVE TOOLS TO CONQUER FEAR

Another effective tool when talking back to that inner voice of hopelessness is to tell the *yetzer hara* that you have heard enough. Let him know that you are in control and that now you want to give the *yetzer tov* a chance to be heard. Use this tool each time fear creates barriers that keep you from moving ahead.

GO OUT AND DO IT

As long as you are progressing in the journey of life there will always be new fears around the corner. It may help to consider that everyone else negotiating unfamiliar territory is also experiencing fear. The only way to get rid of the fear of doing something is to go out and do it. Of course once you have done it the fear disappears. It feels so good to get rid of the fear.

> When the Baal Shem Tov was five years old, he was orphaned from both his father and mother. The last words spoken to him by his holy father before his passing were: "Yisrolik, fear nothing but Hashem alone."
>
> He loved to walk in the fields and in the great, deep forest near his village. From cheder he would make his way to the fields, where he would review by heart what he had learned. Often he would sleep overnight in the field or the forest. Sometimes he would hear terrifying cries in the middle of the night. When this happened and fear would seize him, he would repeat the words of his father to himself again and again (From the writings of Rav Yosef Yitzchok of Lubavitch).

A helpful parable:

> A cheder once took their students to an amusement park. Many of the children chose to ride through the terrifying "Spooky House." They shrank back from the fierce expressions of wild animals and raging witches. The glaring images and petrifying screeches had the children all cowering together in the dark. Their fear was all part of the fun.
>
> There was one child who wasn't enjoying the ride

at all. With every passing moment he became more and more distressed. When a large stack of barrels began to fall, he panicked certain that it was real. By the time the car he was in nearly crashed, he was frantic. He emerged from the ride sickly pale with his hair standing on end.

As soon as he was out, the child began to cry for he had lost his yarmulke in the course of dodging the fearsome apparitions.

"What's the matter," the person in charge asked.

"I dropped my cap."

"No problem, go back inside and get it."

"Absolutely not," the child replied, "I'm not going back in there again."

"Come with me, "the attendant said, entering and flipping the switch. With the lights on, the child saw that what had frightened him were just some colorful pieces of wood.

In real life there is also nothing to fear. All we need to do is turn on the lights of *emunah* so that this fact becomes clear to us (Rabbi Elimelech Biederman).

SET GOALS

GET THINGS DONE

We are in this world to get things done. *Asher bara Elokim la'asos*—"and Hashem created to do" (*Bereishis* 2:3). Hashem created us to do, to strive to accomplish. That is our task.

One either goes forward or goes backward in life. Of course, everyone wants to progress. You might get the general overall impression that you are moving in the right direction, but that may be just an illusion. Without goals, you have no focus. You are simply floating around, unable to channel your efforts effectively. Setting meaningful goals forces you to crystallize and articulate the desires floating in your mind.

GOALS HELP YOU LIVE WITH MORE AWARENESS

When you do not have goals, you will often find yourself

getting sidetracked. Goals ensure that you are channeling your time, energy and efforts into things that really matter to you. They help you live more consciously.

Imagine receiving a jigsaw puzzle as a gift. Before you can open it your younger brother has spilled out all the pieces on the table. Eager to get started, you reach for the box so that you can see what you are meant to put together. To your dismay, the top of the box is blank. There's no picture. How will you manage to put the puzzle together if you have no guidelines? Without an idea of what the final image should look like, you have no idea where to begin.

 Food For Thought

When we do not focus and refocus on our goals we can end up like the person who gets on a train going in the wrong direction. When he is informed that he is on the wrong train, he gets up and changes his seat so that he faces his destination. But of course he is still traveling in the wrong direction (Rav Yozel of Novardock).

EXAMINE YOUR GOALS

Start by deciding which goal is important to you. The benefits of your goals have to be clear – only then can you keep on track if the going gets rough. Fix in your mind what you hope to accomplish. Be specific. Focus on what you are going to do, not what you are not going to do. Whatever your goal is, break it down into daily and weekly sub-goals.

Determine what you intend to invest in to reach your goal. Establish a definite period to accomplish your goal. Create a plan in writing that includes back-up alternate routes. Ask yourself how you are planning to get to your destination. What are the choices you have to deal with? Then begin at once. Read your statement daily. Strengthen your commitment by sharing your goal with your friends. This way you will be forced into a framework of accountability.

POSSIBLE GOALS

Maybe you aspire to *daven* with more *kavanah*. Perhaps your ambition is to excel at school. Perhaps you want to invest in friendship and the growth that it engenders. People of accomplishment do not let things happen to them, they go out and happen to things. Identify your resources. There can never be a better time than now.

 Ask Yourself:

What is my current goal?

How much of my energy have I wasted through being overly cautious?

Are my goals an expression of any form of *gaivah*?

A girl read about a woman who changed her cloth-ing from casual to dress when it came time to daven Minchah. Inspired, she wanted to do something similar. "Is it a good idea for me to put on my Shabbos shoes whenever I daven?" she asked her rav.

His response took her breath away. "Only until you begin to think you are better than others who do not do so."

The importance of small steps.

Rav Elyah Lopian encouraged his students to take on one or two goals at a time. When they shared their goals with him, he would suggest they shrink their undertak-ing and break their goals into smaller pieces. Sometimes he would repeat that suggestion until they reached a more manageable goal.

VISUALIZE REACHING YOUR GOAL

THINK ABOUT WHO YOU WANT TO BE

Take time to concentrate your thoughts daily on considering the individual you intend to become so that you create a clear mental picture of that person in your mind. Ask yourself what changes you need to make to get closer to your objectives. Try to identify any hurdles that are stopping you. These may be either inner or external obstacles.

FIND SOMEONE WHO INSPIRES YOU

Try to find someone who inspires you. It can be someone

with the kind of joyous *simchas ha'chayim* or confidence you aspire to. You may choose someone who is very organized or someone who is a serious student (Piasetzna Rebbe). Truthfully, almost anyone can be an inspiration to you. Inspiration will nourish the day-to-day work of trying to reach your goals.

IF YOU CAN IMAGINE IT YOU CAN CREATE IT

Imagine yourself as the best you can possibly be and then transform yourself into that image. Visualize the full life you will have, with Hashem's help, when you reach your goal. Create a mental picture with as many details as you can muster. Feel free to fill in and add to your picture. Your only restrictions are the limits of your imagination. If you are able to imagine it, then you can create it. It's okay to alter the details as long as you keep moving ahead. Arrange old concepts, ideas or plans into new combinations, expand your vision of what is possible but keep going.

Goals help you get up in the morning. They allow you to stretch yourself in the process of acquiring new tools. The energy created by the clear visualization of your goals actually helps you get there. Your efforts and hard work will be converted into pleasures as you discover what you can really accomplish.

> A depressed Torah scholar visited the Steipler for encouragement and advice. "When a person doesn't have a goal he becomes depressed," the Steipler told him. "A person has to have something to get up for in the morning." He thought for a moment. "Why don't you write a sefer?" he advised. The Torah scholar followed the Steipler's advice and his depression disappeared.

The Piasetzna Rebbe helped his students create long and short term goals for themselves. Knowing that the best way to reach a goal is by striving for an even more ambitious goal, the rebbe would constantly raise the bar on the long-term goals. He suggested that they choose a person who had successfully reached their specific goal so that they could measure their attainments against the achievements of their role model.

Ask Yourself:

What outcome am I looking for?

Have I tried reaching this goal to my best ability?

Have I procrastinated or have I been persistent?

Food For Thought

"When I was young I was sure that I would rise to Heaven in a whirlwind like Eliyahu the prophet. Now that I am old, I have given up on that dream. I have only one *tefillah* now; that I won't have to endure *gehinom*. But without those youthful aspirations who knows where I would be now" (Rav Yitzchok Isaac of Komarna).

Someone once commented to the Ponovitcher Rav, who built so many dynamic Torah institutions in his life, how fortunate he was to have accomplished so much compared to the average person who only ac-complishes about 10 percent of what they set out to do. His response was, "I have also only accomplished about 10 percent of what I set out to do, but I set out to do a lot more than the average person."

THE KEY TO SUCCESS

TOTAL FOCUS

Perhaps you have noticed that the only place success comes before work is in the dictionary. Experts in every area have one thing in common. They are completely taken up with their field of endeavor. They are not afraid of difficult tasks although they are realistic about what they take on.

THE VALUE OF RESEARCH

Definite longings, together with hard work lead to excellence, with Hashem's help. To do anything well you have to research, watch others, improve and repeat. Open your mind to new information and new points of view. Thomas Edison, the inventor of the light bulb, learned all that he could from other scientists and researchers. He used that information to develop a number of inventions.

ASSUME A SELF-CONFIDENT POSTURE

You don't need to feel self-confident to speak and act with self-confidence. Assuming a self-confident posture will eventually fill you with self-confidence. Sometimes you succeed and other times you learn. If you do not have time to do it right, how will you have the time to do it over?

AVOID PERFECTIONISM

Excellence is not perfectionism. Perfectionism is sacrificing yourself to the imagined demands of internal demons or indifferent outsiders. It is the enemy of accomplishment. It doesn't allow you to move on. Excellence is grounded within, and involves using the unique talents Hashem has given you. Don't allow yourself to be hindered by your insecure need to do what everyone else is doing, which might not necessarily be good for you.

DO WHAT IS RIGHT

People of excellence go the extra mile to do what's right. The more they do what is right the greater they become. The greater they become the better they feel about themselves. Your life is the accumulation of the good things you have done.

Ask yourself at least once a week:

"Am I on the right track to achieve my goals at this time?

Am I doing things that will bring me closer to where I want to be?"

FOCUS ON ONE OR TWO THINGS AT A TIME

Ideally, you want to focus on one or at most two things and do them well. Undertaking too much, means not getting enough sleep and being overly stressed out. This in turn will decrease your ability to function. You're either going to do a couple of things well, or do lots of things poorly.

"WHEN ONE TAKES ACTION TO ACCOMPLISH ANYTHING, HE MUST STRENGTHEN HIMSELF STILL MORE IN EMUNAH. AND, WHEN ONE'S EFFORTS RESULT IN SUCCESS, THEN HE MUST START WORKING ON STRENGTHENING HIS EMUNAH EVEN MORE" (MIDRASH PINCHAS).

KEEP REMINDING YOURSELF THAT HASHEM ALONE DIRECTS EVERYTHING

One must believe with pure faith that Hashem alone directs everything, and that there is no other cause for what happens. Being connected to a wellspring of faith and *bitachon* enables a person to optimally fulfill the unique tasks that each and every individual has in life. You will be able to take action while fully aware that Hashem is pulling the strings.

When Rav Naftali Tzvi Yehudah Berlin, known as the Netziv, published his sefer Ha'amek Sheilah *he invited a few Torah scholars to his house to celebrate the event. When they were sitting around the table the Netziv said, "You are probably wondering why I called you together at this time. I will be happy to explain why this is a cause for celebration.*

"When I was a child, I was a very weak student. One day I heard my father discussing my progress with my mother. I heard him say with great pain in his voice, 'I always hoped that Naftal Tzvi would grow up to be a great Torah scholar. But apparently it was not meant to be. We will have to content ourselves with him being a working man who will hopefully involve himself in helping others.'

"When I heard those words," the Netziv continued, "my father's pain touched my heart. I decided that I would try my utmost to succeed at my learning. I ran into the room where my parents were talking and informed them of my decision. In truth, from that day onward, I never let up. I studied with enthusiasm without wasting any time. Hashem helped and I succeeded beyond my wildest dreams.

"If you ask me," the Netziv continued, "What is the connection between this story and the current celebration? I will explain. Imagine what would have happened if I had never overheard that conversation and undertaken to become a Torah scholar. I would have lived the life of a good Jew. I might have become a tailor or a carpenter. I would have certainly designated some time each day for Torah studies. But just imagine what would have happened the day I died. I would be asked, 'Did you set aside time for Torah study?' Of course, I would have answered yes. I would have explained how I devoted the rest of my day to my work and various good deeds.

"Then the Creator would have produced the books, 'Ha'amek Sheilah', 'Meromei Sadeh' and 'Ha'amek Davar' and would say to me, 'You had the ability to write these seforim. Where did they go?' Woe to the embarrassment I would have endured. That is why I am overjoyed. I made a commitment, a commitment which elevated me to Torah greatness. This is a great day for me."

A young boy decides, "I can do it." This decision enables him to become the great Rosh Yeshivah of Volozhin.

YOU ARE A WINNER

YOU ARE SUCCESSFUL IN MANY WAYS

Remember that success is not a destination. It is a road you are already walking on, for now as you read these words you are successful in many ways. You have many winning personal qualities that make you great. By reading this book you demonstrate that you are a winner who is working on doing things the right way and striving to become a person of value.

Exercise

Make a list of qualities that you like about yourself. When a difficult situation arises, read your list.

SPEND TIME WITH PEOPLE WHO BELIEVE IN YOU

We have the ability to choose our thoughts. Don't make the mistake of underestimating yourself. Spend time with people who believe in you. Try to see yourself as they see you. When they are unavailable, imagine a coach whispering inspiring messages in your ear. "You can do what you set out to do! It's easier than you think."

WORK ON PATIENCE AND DELIBERATION

If you are aware of your strengths and areas of accomplishment, you will achieve even more. Successful people are not necessarily more capable than unsuccessful people, but they are not as readily discouraged. Patience and deliberation are essential qualities which are the seal of a wise man.

> There was a caliph who had two sons, from two different wives: One son was the crown prince, his queen's child. The other son's mother was one of his other wives. One day the caliph noticed that the queen was crying. When he asked her why she was crying, she responded, "I couldn't help noticing that the maidservant's son is always in your chambers. It hurts me to see that you favor that son over mine."
>
> The caliph replied, "You are right; forgive me. Send for your son, and I will begin by asking him to do something for me." When her son appeared, the caliph said to him, "Go to the store and bring me some threads." The boy bowed to his father the caliph, and set out immediately to do his bidding.
>
> When the shopkeeper asked him what type of threads he required, he did not know. He had forgotten to ask the

caliph. Upon returning, the caliph instructed him regarding the threads' texture. The boy returned to the store only to be asked what colors the caliph wanted. Once again, the boy had no answer. He felt ashamed for not asking the color before he left. The caliph instructed him to purchase white threads. He returned to the store only to be questioned regarding the amount of the threads the caliph required. Embarrassed by his ignorance, the boy returned to the caliph at which point the caliph told him he no longer needed the threads.

Afterwards, the caliph instructed his aide to call the other wife's son. When the boy arrived, the caliph asked him to purchase threads for him. The boy immediately responded, "Father, what type of threads do you want: wool or linen, thick or thin, what color and how many? Perhaps if you tell me for what purpose these threads will be used, I can purchase the ones most appropriate." The caliph now turned to the queen and said, "Do you now understand why I favor this son?"

One should not move ahead without considering all the options. Knowing what to ask and how to question is a sign of wisdom (Nachlas Tzvi).

THE QUESTIONS A WINNER ASKS HIMSELF

When you find yourself agonizing over a problem, consider if it is really worth all the emotional energy you are investing. Reorient yourself, and instead of getting upset, decide to use the challenge. Don't say, "Why must I go through this?" Instead, ask yourself, "What can I do to improve the situation? How should I respond to this? How can I become a better person through this challenge?" A winner finds it difficult to quit. He keeps on problem solving, considering all kinds of solutions until he gets it right, until he reaches that wonderful high that accompanies a goal achieved.

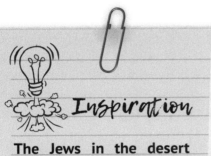

Inspiration

The Jews in the desert had never worked with anything other than brick and mortar. When the time came to build the *Mishkan*, the untrained volunteers did not say, "There's no way we can do this." They were so enthusiastic about building the *Mishkan* that they declared, "We will do whatever we're asked." They discovered an important fact: There is no limit to what a person can do when he believes in himself (Rav Chaim Shmulevitz).

"WORSE THAN THE PERSON WHO'S UNAWARE OF HIS DEFECTS IS THE PERSON WHO IS UNAWARE OF HIS STRENGTHS, FOR HE LACKS THE BASIC TOOLS WITH WHICH TO SERVE HASHEM" (RAV YERUCHAM LEVOVITZ).

IF YOU THINK YOU CAN SUCCEED, YOU'RE PROVIDING THE VESSEL FOR YOUR SUCCESS, INCREASING THE CHANCE OF ITS MATERIALIZATION (RAMBAN).

A gadol ha'dor told the following story about himself:

No one ever thought that I would amount to much. Accidents followed me everywhere. When my teacher asked me for a cup of tea, I was trembling so hard that the glass slipped off the tray, to the great amusement of my classmates.

I really tried hard. Each year brought fresh opportunities to begin a new page. Unfortunately, all my attempts ended in failure. My parents lost all hope. The future looked bleak. I was in the pit of despair.

One year we had a teacher with a warm heart and a lot of enthusiasm. He believed that concealed within each of his students were great talents and abilities. All he needed to do was to reveal our hidden potential. He decided to invest his main efforts in the class problem. He directed his attention to me. The very first day he asked that I bring 10 glasses of tea into a room where several teachers were meeting.

"Don't you know that I am the ultimate klutz?" I said softly with my eyes lowered.

He didn't budge, "My dear student, I need ten cups of tea within five minutes."

As I filled the cups with hot water, I looked around for the mop and schmattes. I thought to myself, "The best way to minimize my embarrassment is to walk very slowly." I managed to get out of the teacher's room safely. I couldn't believe my good luck. I carefully walked towards the table where my teacher was seated. When I bent down to place the tray on the desk, two cups of tea fell right onto the legs of one of the teachers. His yelps could be heard down the hall.

I ran out as quickly as my legs could carry me. Suddenly I felt a gentle hand on my trembling shoulders. "I told you," I blurted out when I saw my teacher's face. He didn't look upset. "It's not as bad as you think. Remember you successfully served eight glasses of tea.

"Tomorrow I want you to get yourself a rubber band large enough to go around your wrist. Every time you begin to feel like a certified failure, pull the rubber band and let it go. When it smacks your wrist, you will be prompted to switch tracks. Instead of seeing yourself in a negative light, take a moment to reinterpret the situation in a positive way. For example if you are learning and having a hard time understanding the gemara you are studying, before you despair pull on the band. This will remind you to stop and take control of your thoughts."

The first days of that experiment my hand was red and bruised from the constant twangs of the band. Soon enough I got used to thinking along positive lines. As a result, my self-confidence shot up. It did not even take that long for me to actually see results. Since success breeds success, in a short time the klutz who would never amount to much disappeared.

Now when I look back at those years of difficulties and hopelessness I thank Hashem for having sent me a messenger to facilitate my ability to use the natural talents that Hashem had given me. I learned that if a person wishes he can use his talents to scale the heights. There is only one prerequisite and that is to believe in yourself (Sheifos).

DON'T GIVE UP

FAILURE AND SUCCESS ARE IN THE HANDS OF HASHEM

Failure and success is from Hashem. The more you ask of Hashem the greater will be your recognition of this basic fact. Nothing is in your power but the choices and efforts that you make toward the ultimate goal of spiritual worthiness. Keep checking to make sure that you are moving towards that goal.

"VE'HAAKSHAN YATZLIACH—
THE STUBBORN ONE
WILL SUCCEED"

(RAV CHAIM VOLOZHINER).

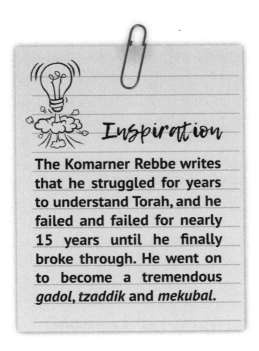

Inspiration

The Komarner Rebbe writes that he struggled for years to understand Torah, and he failed and failed for nearly 15 years until he finally broke through. He went on to become a tremendous *gadol*, *tzaddik* and *mekubal*.

NEVER MISTAKE TEMPORARY DEFEAT FOR TOTAL FAILURE

It's a mistake to believe that only a person who is always successful is worthy. When you are confronted with failure, don't forget who you are: a pure soul, a child of Hashem both in success and failure. Easy successes are not necessarily positive. They usually grant only superficial happiness. You can accomplish so much

> *"WHEN HASHEM SEES A PERSON WHO PERSISTS DESPITE HIS FAILURES, HE SHAPES THOSE FAILURES INTO FUTURE SUCCESS"*
>
> (ERECH APAYIM).

if you don't take disappointments seriously. Never mistake temporary defeat for total failure. No person is a failure until he accepts failure as a reality in his own mind, for it is giving up that makes failure permanent. A flop is temporary but quitting is difficult to reverse.

 Do not label yourself as "stupid" or "incompetent". Instead, tell yourself, "I made a mistake. Next time, I'll do better."

Many who abandon hope do not realize how close they were to success when they gave up.

 ## Food For Thought

R.U. Darby caught the "gold fever" in the gold-rush days. He staked a claim and went to work. After weeks of labor he discovered the shining ore. He returned to Maryland and told his relatives and few neighbors about his "strike". Catching the Darby's enthusiasm, they took their savings and borrowed what was needed to buy tools and machinery, enabling Darby and his uncle to get quickly back to work. The first car of ore was mined and shipped. The quality of the ore proved that they had one of the richest mines in Colorado! To their distress however, when their drills went back down for more, the vein of gold ore disappeared. They drilled on desperately trying to pick up the vein again but failed.

They decided to quit. They sold the machinery to a junk man and took the train back home. But the junk man was intrigued. He called in a mining engineer who calculated that the gold vein continued on about three feet from where the Darbys had stopped drilling. He withdrew millions of dollars in ore from the mine. He was wise enough to seek expert advice before giving up.

Reb Moshe Leib of Sassov once traveled from one city to the next, trying to collect money to ransom Jews from debtor's prison. He did not succeed in gathering the required sum. His regret was compounded by the thought of how much time had been wasted from Torah study and tefillah. In the future, he resolved, he would remain at home.

On that same day, he heard about a Jew who had been caught stealing and had been beaten and jailed for his crime. Reb Moshe Leib interceded with the judge to gain the thief's release.

When the tzaddik went to fetch the thief from jail, he warned him, "Remember the beating they gave you and don't ever do anything like that again."

"Why not" asked the thief. "If you don't succeed the first time, you may succeed the next."

"If that is the case," thought Reb Moshe Leib, "then I must keep trying at my job too" (Mipi Chassidim).

The importance of trying again.

The Yesod Ha'avodah of Slonim once asked a chassid.

"How did you get here?"

"By donkey," he replied.

"And if you would have fallen off the donkey, what would you have done?"

"I would have gotten back on the donkey and continued on my way."

"And if you had fallen down again, then what?"

"I would again have gotten back on my donkey, and continued my journey."

"And would you continue on if you fell off a third time?" the rebbe insisted.

"Rebbe," the chassid said, "What is my alternative? I certainly would not sit on the ground and cry! I would mount the donkey again."

The rebbe turned to his chassidim, "No matter how many times you fall down, keep lifting yourselves up again, and try again."

FAILURE AS A SPRINGBOARD TO SUCCESS

REMAIN POSITIVE

The journey of life is littered with pitfalls, with hundreds of disappointments. As the years pass, the memories fade away and are forgotten. Since they cannot be avoided, it makes sense to accept them with a positive attitude, for they can be quite useful. Every failure brings with it the seed of success.

MOST DEFEAT IS TEMPORARY

Most defeat is temporary. If plan A doesn't work there

are twenty five additional letters. When you look around and see success stories, you may not find out about the temporary defeats that they had to surmount before "arriving".

- Just when the caterpillar thought his world was ending, he turned into a butterfly.
- Abraham Lincoln lost every election he ran for except for the last one.
- Thomas A. Edison "failed" ten thousand times before he perfected the incandescent electric light bulb. He met with temporary defeat ten thousand times before his efforts were crowned with success.

> "A PERSON IS A SUCCESS WHEN HE MASTERS THE TRAIT OF SINCERELY REJOICING AT THE SUCCESS OF OTHERS"
>
> (RAV YECHEZKEL LEVENSTEIN).

GENERATING THRUST

When one wants to take a great jump, he will generate thrust by stepping backwards and then sprinting forward. The momentum helps him jump higher. It is the same before rising to a higher spiritual level; one needs to move backwards and then leap. Although you might feel like you are falling, this fall will lead to growth (Rabbi Baruch of Mezibuz).

FAILURE MEANS IT'S RECALCULATING TIME

Feeling secure in our essential worth will make it easier for us to face up to our errors before we move on. A person with good self-esteem who fails at something will take his failure in stride and view his failures as a temporary setback. Failure ought to be a "learning experience." It means that your plan must be tweaked. Accept is as a signal that you must reevaluate what you are currently doing, try to work out what went wrong, adjust your plan and then try again. It may require harder, longer or smarter techniques. It may mean re-evaluating your goal and the method you have chosen to attain it.

GET GOOD ADVICE

Have you sought advice? The biggest and the best consult with others, we surely need to do so. There is a big difference between giving up and re-charting your course. Once you have recalculated get back on track moving towards your desired goal.

Increase your *tefillos*. Internalize your dependence on Hashem and move on.

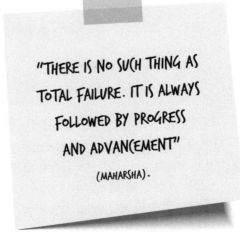

"THERE IS NO SUCH THING AS TOTAL FAILURE. IT IS ALWAYS FOLLOWED BY PROGRESS AND ADVANCEMENT"

(MAHARSHA).

When You Hit A Brick Wall Ask Yourself:

Is what I am doing working? Could I be doing it better? Is there something that I should stop doing?

Harav Pam once lost a job at the last minute to another candidate. It was a position teaching Spanish. Then he ultimately became Rosh Yeshivah of Torah Vodaas. So very different from the career trajectory that he "lost" when the teaching opportunity was snatched from him.

"THE LETDOWN WHICH FOLLOWS FAILURE COMPELS THE PERSON TO UNDERTAKE SELF-IMPROVEMENT"

(RAV CHAIM SHMULEVITZ).

Yankel the water carrier had two buckets connected to the yoke across his shoulders. One pail was cracked; the other was whole. Each day he would fill the buckets with water. By the time he arrived at his destination, the water in the cracked bucket had slowly seeped out so *there was only a bit left.*

One day, the cracked bucket turned to Yankel and said, "I'm ashamed of myself! I want to apologize to you."

"Why?" Yankel asked.

"I'm ashamed of the cracks that allow the water to escape, depriving you of your well-deserved pay."

Yankel looked at the bucket with compassion and said, "You're making a very big mistake." As they walked the path leading from the well to town, Yankel said, "Look at your side."

The bucket saw a magnificent garden of blossoms.

"Now look at the other side," Yankel said.

The side through which the whole bucket has passed had only rocks and sparse grass.

"Who do you think is responsible for this scenic path?!" Yankel asked. "For the past two years, you have been watering these delightful flowers, and know that they are collected to adorn many homes in the city."

THE GIFT OF TESHUVAH

THE TESHUVAH PROCESS IS SO CLEANSING

There is nothing more uplifting than the *teshuvah* process. It is so cleansing. In the opening words of *Shaarei Teshuvah*, Rabbeinu Yona reminds us that one of the great gifts given to us by Hashem is *teshuvah*. As Dovid *Ha'melech* writes, "Because Hashem is good and just; He teaches the sinners the right way" (*Tehillim* 25:8). Hashem has given us the guidance we require to uproot our sin and rescue ourselves before the punishment begins.

TESHUVAH RAISES YOU TO THE HIGHEST HEAVEN

When you realize that you have done something wrong

and resolve to do *teshuvah*, you rise immediately to the highest Heaven, to the very presence of the Throne of Glory (Pesikta Rabbasi). Hashem will respond with boundless compassion for we have cut ourselves loose from the category of sinner and pasted ourselves into the category of righteous. The Chasam Sofer emphasizes that this tactic works even when a person's sins have taken him to a terrible place. All he has to do is reorient himself and Hashem grants His forgiveness, as Dovid Ha'melech wrote, *Derachok mizrach mimaarav hirchik mimenu es peshaeinu*—"As far as the east is from the west so far has Hashem removed from us our transgressions" (*Tehillim* 103: 12).

YOU ARE RECREATED BY TESHUVAH

There is no sin that cannot be mended and remedied by *teshuvah*. The best part about *teshuvah* is that it transforms an action that created a break in our relationship with Hashem into an agent of even greater connection to Him and ultimately

"A PERSON REMAINS IN HIS ELEVATED POSITION EVEN WHEN HE SINS, AND WITH EVERY SIN, A PERSON HAS THE OPPORTUNITY TO LEARN A LESSON AND CLIMB EVEN HIGHER" (ALTER OF SLOBODKA).

"IF YOU BELIEVE THAT YOU ARE ABLE TO RUIN THINGS, THEN BELIEVE THAT YOU ARE ABLE TO FIX THEM" (LIKUTEI MOHARAN).

to more *mitzvos*! It is electrifying to recreate yourself and actually watch your defects disappear.

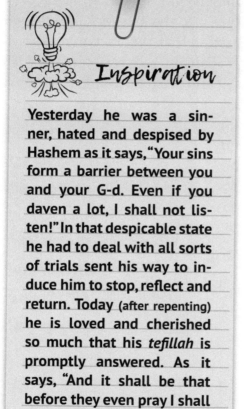

Inspiration

Yesterday he was a sinner, hated and despised by Hashem as it says, "Your sins form a barrier between you and your G-d. Even if you daven a lot, I shall not listen!" In that despicable state he had to deal with all sorts of trials sent his way to induce him to stop, reflect and return. Today (after repenting) **he is loved and cherished so much that his *tefillah* is promptly answered. As it says, "And it shall be that before they even pray I shall answer"** (Hilchos Teshuvah).

When Reb Boruch Ber of Kamenitz's father took ill, he sat at his father's bedside for countless days and nights. His students, fearful for his health, insisted that they could take over. He finally agreed to leave his father's bedside a few hours a day.

Shortly thereafter his father died. Reb Boruch Ber was hounded by the concern that he had not properly honored his father. The distress so devastated him that he had to stop giving his regular Torah lectures. He took advantage of a meeting of prominent rabbis in Vilna to pour out his heart to the Chofetz Chaim. The Chofetz Chaim spoke to him at length about the power of repentance. He stressed that teshuvah not only atones for the sin, but actually transforms the baal teshuvah into a different person entirely. That

longer has a connection to the past one. Reb Boruch
Ber later said, "The Chofetz Chaim revived my spirit"
(Ha'rav Domeh Le'malach, pp. 310-311).

EVERYONE HAS BAD DAYS

SEIZE THE HAPPY MOMENTS

Some days everything seems to go wrong. Your favorite sweater was in the hamper. Someone borrowed your hairbrush and you couldn't find it. When you picked up your school bag the strap tore and the books and papers flew all over the place. At school some of your friends left you out of their conversations. You said something to a teacher that you later regretted. You spoke badly about a friend. Your performance was not as good as it could have been.

When your mood turns despondent, and it feels like a "bad day," focus on the knowledge that every day really has a lot of good in it; on some days, you just have to work a little harder to see it. Your mood improves and deteriorates in turn, even on the most difficult of days. The trick is to seize the happier moments and highlight the positive. Use that affirmative energy to do something encouraging for someone. Such activities go a long way in lighting up your day.

RECORD YOUR ACCOMPLISHMENTS

It is valuable to keep a mental photo album of good memories so that when things aren't going well, you can recall them. Even better, designate a section in a notebook to record your accomplishments throughout the course of the day, however minor they may seem. It helps to put together a list of all your strong points: intellectual, physical, emotional and spiritual. Consult periodically for motivation. Refer to as needed.

> "ALL OF US HAVE OUR WEAKNESSES, BUT YOU MUST BE AWARE THAT THEY DON'T PREVENT US FROM ACCOMPLISHING GREAT THINGS" (SHEIFOS).

WE ALL NEED *KAPARAH*

Remember no one is perfect. We all need *kaparah* for the negative things we do. Hashem is constantly testing us to determine how clearly we see that He is in charge. Your reaction to the irritations He sends your way broadcast what you are thinking and feeling inside.

WHAT HAVE YOU GAINED?

When something goes wrong, instead of feeling overwhelmed, you can ask yourself if there is something you have gained from this situation. It might be patience, humility, generosity or perseverance. Has it made you a better person? When things do not go smoothly, it may be that you lack the information, skill, or experience to do better. Lacking certain skills does not make you a failure. Everyone has areas of deficiency but this does not detract from their value.

> "REFLECT ON YOUR DAY AND HOW IT WENT WRONG. CONSIDER WHERE YOU COULD HAVE RECALCULATED TO PREVENT THINGS FROM GOING DOWNHILL"
>
> (REBBE NACHMAN).

> "NO ONE KNOWS HOW MANY BATTLES THE CHOFETZ CHAIM FOUGHT AND HOW MANY SPIRITUAL HARDSHIPS HE HAD TO OVERCOME UNTIL HE ACHIEVED HIS GREATNESS IN TORAH AND MIDDOS"
>
> (RAV HUTNER).

THERE ARE GRAND OPPORTUNITIES AHEAD

Sometimes it is feelings that distress us. It can be feelings of anger or jealousy that can drag us to a bad place. It takes time to sort out the triggers and move away from the anguish. The good part is you get another chance tomorrow. A good night's sleep can be really healing and return your brighter view of life. In the morning when you say *Modeh Ani* thank Hashem for another opportunity. Reassure yourself that this new day will be full of grand opportunities.

A prominent Rosh Yeshivah experienced emotional difficulties as a yeshivah boy. At one point, he felt that he had reached a breaking point. He could no longer continue dealing with his problems alone. He poured out his anguished heart to his rebbe, Rav Shlomo Zalmen Auerbach.

Rav Shlomo Zalmen replied, "Did you ever see a tailor at work? He takes a beautiful piece of fabric and cuts it into pieces large and small. A person with limited experience might shout at the tailor for destroying the piece of fabric. 'Wait and you will the see the handsome final result.' The tailor would respond.

"The tailor starts connecting the pieces and in a short time you can actually see the suit taking shape."

After he finished the parable, he asked his student, "Can the tailor sew up a beautiful garment without destroying the fabric?"

The bachur replied, "Of course not! It can't be done!"

Rav Shlomo Zalmen smiled, "It is the same with these low periods that you are experiencing; they will propel you upwards. It is the equivalent of cutting up the fabric to create an elevated spiritual suit. It is not possible to create a 'superior man' without these crisis the likes of which you are now enduring" (Sheifos).

DON'T COMPLAIN

FOCUS ON THE POSITIVE

You may find yourself moving from positive to negative and back again several times in the course of a single day. The challenge is where your focus lies. You need to focus on the more pleasant aspects of life, not on the bumps in the road. You will then be able to convert pleasant events into happy energy for upcoming days.

 Tell yourself each day that Hashem wants you to be happy.

LOOK FOR SOLUTIONS

Our grumbling is usually directed at the wrong people and rarely improves things. Instead of pointing the finger at other people, use it to find a new solution. Instead of complaining, improve the situation by saying and doing something positive, that will make things better. Avoid excuses that lay the blame on others such as: "It's not my fault." If something is bothering you and it can't be fixed, accept the fact that nothing can be done right now.

JUDGE FAVORABLY

It is likely that you complain about others because you think they are not up to your standards or you are annoyed that they are not complying with your request. Once you realize that you do not really know each person's real story, you will stop judging people and complain less about the things they do.

WOULD YOU RATHER COMPLAIN OR BE HAPPY?

After all, the more you complain, the unhappier you get. Ask yourself if you would rather complain or be happy? The best you can do is to change the way you think about it. This requires practice but it is worth the effort. When you find yourself thinking or saying a negative comment about something, stop and force yourself to say something positive instead. Enlist the help of a positive, optimistic friend to stop you when you complain and help you to see the positive in the

"EVERYONE PASSES THROUGH THIS WORLD EITHER IN JOY OR IN SADNESS. WE CAN'T CHANGE WHAT WILL HAPPEN. BUT WE CAN BENEFIT BY PASSING THROUGH WITH JOY" ((HAZON ISH).

situation. If you learn to stop complaining, you will see your life changing for the better.

Exercise

Get yourself a giant rubber band that fits comfortably on your wrist and is easy to remove. Every time you find yourself complaining about something, take it off and move it to the other hand. Do the same every time you find yourself appreciating something in your life. This little technique will help you become aware of your daily thoughts and allow you to introduce more thoughts that are positive into your repertoire.

HASHEM HAS GIVEN US SO MUCH

If you find yourself about to complain, think of your many blessings and rejoice! Imagine being served a six-course meal at a friend's house. When it is time for dessert, your host abruptly informs you that the meal is over. Can you imagine becoming morally indignant, pounding on the table and demanding dessert? Of course not! After all, you are only a guest in someone else's home, and you have already received so much! In the same vein, our reaction to a difficult event should be tempered by the fact that Hashem loves us and has already given us so much (Rabbi Manis Friedman).

Rav Schwadron told a story that took place when he was visiting the home of a frum man. His host wanted to spend some time at the beach. In preparation, he called to inquire about the weather conditions at the seashore. To his disappointment he discovered that access to the ocean was forbidden due to high winds.

Rav Schwadron commented, "You will not believe me but the man's face took on dark overtones. The look on his face shouted 'suffering!' He sighed a great sigh and cried out, 'Oy, Ribono Shel Olam, see my suffering and allow it to atone for my sins'" (Zekeinecha ve'yomri lach, page 144).

Rav Schwadron was horrified at how this man treated a minor disappointment as if it were a major catastrophe.

A group of women came to Rebbetzin Sarah Kramer to ask for her blessing. In the course of their conversation, one woman asked how she could be happy while she waited for the blessing to materialize.

The childless Rebbetzin – who had suffered in Auschwitz from the experiments of Dr. Mengele, the notorious "Angel of Death" – was surprised by the question. "You have eyes and they see," she replied in puzzlement. "You have ears and they hear. You have feet and they take you wherever you want to go. How can you not be happy?"

THINK POSITIVE

OUR PERSONAL WEALTH IS EXTRAORDINARY

Our personal wealth is extraordinary. Consider the following; you are alive! You have so many internal resources. Most of us have family, health and so much more. And even those who do not have a normal family or health situation, are getting help and medication, etc. You live in a country where you can perform Hashem's *mitzvos* without interference. Each one of you could add so much to this list!

> "WHEN A PERSON FOCUSES ON THE POSITIVE IN A DIFFICULT SITUATION, HE CONVERTS THE DIFFICULTY TO SALVATION"
>
> (DEGEL MACHANE EPHRAIM).

ENJOY WHAT YOU HAVE

It is not the absence of something that makes you feel unhappy; it is your inability to accept what you don't have that can make you so miserable. There are those who fail to enjoy what they have, because they long for what they lack. It is clear that there is no limit to what one doesn't have. These intense feelings are simply a result of the fact that you live in a world dominated by advertising that constantly teases you, and forces you to focus on all the things you don't have - and tells you how happy you would be, with yourself and your life, if only you owned their product. It takes concentrated effort to resist these messages, but it can be done.

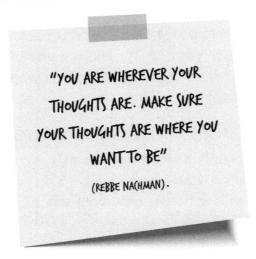

"YOU ARE WHEREVER YOUR THOUGHTS ARE. MAKE SURE YOUR THOUGHTS ARE WHERE YOU WANT TO BE"

(REBBE NACHMAN).

SMALL CHANGES MAKE US FEEL GREAT

If the focus of your life is on not having, then unsurprisingly your life is full of never-ending unhappiness. You have the power to let the bad feelings go by focusing on what you have and not what you lack. Even small changes in thinking have the power to make us feel great.

 Try at least once a day to replace wanting with thanking.

REPLACE NEGATIVE THOUGHTS WITH POSITIVE ONES

If you find yourself thinking negative thoughts, tell your-self calmly to stop. Put together a list of positive thoughts that can be played back in moments of crisis. Thinking happy thoughts can be inspiring and empowering. They can provide support anytime and anywhere.

If your friend moves away, instead of concluding that you are doomed to a life of loneliness, focus on the fact that you have space in your life for another good friend. Added bonus: you will learn about a new place when you call or visit your old friend.

MAKE THE MOST OF EVERY SITUATION

If you have only a small role in a play, make the most of your part and do your absolute best. The extra-curricular coordinator will be noting how well you handled the part you received and will certainly want to work with you on future projects. The others will be impressed by your mid-dos, and the entire atmosphere will be uplifted.

If you are unhappy because you didn't get the room-mates you wanted, make it your business to be nice to the roommates you received. Assume they want to be friendly as well. You may just make a friend for a lifetime.

Ask Yourself:

"What am I telling myself about this occurrence to make myself sad?"

Rabbi Noach Weinberg had a student named Daniel who had only one leg, yet he was always joyous. Once Rabbi Weinberg approached Daniel and asked that he share the secret of his happiness.

Daniel told the following story;

"When I was nine years old, I was run over by a truck while I was riding my bicycle. I was taken straight to the operating room where the doctors tried to reattach my leg, but they were unsuccessful.

"I remember awakening in the children's ward of the hospital, surrounded by other children who had also suffered severe injuries. I was there for weeks as I slowly recovered.

"My bed was near the door, and one day I overheard two doctors discussing the children in the room.

"'That boy in the corner lost both legs in a traffic accident.'

"'What happened to that teenaged girl who was blinded?'

"'She's in surgery right now, but apparently it's hopeless.'

"They discussed one serious case after another. Finally, they started talking about my own case. It took me a moment to realize they were discussing me, but

once I recognized the details of my own accident, I called out, 'I've only lost one leg, but other than that, I'm fine!'

"The moment I blurted out those words, I felt as if a light had been opened in a very dark room. Yes, I had suffered the loss of a leg, but the rest of me was fine. I had my arms. I could see. I had everything, in fact, except for one leg. I realized that I should be grateful and happy, not bitter and upset. That was when I learned the secret of happiness" (A Midrash and a Maaseh).

THIS TOO IS FOR THE GOOD

EVERYTHING DECREED BY HASHEM IS FOR YOUR BENEFIT

Recognize that Hashem orchestrates every event in this world and that everything decreed by Hashem is for your benefit. Everything that comes from Heaven is good. Whatever is given or not given is all for the good. If we no longer have something, or never had it in the first place, that is a clear indication that we don't need it and are better off without it.

Look for the good in every situation and every encounter. Every adversity has the seed of great benefit stored within. Set your mind on noticing the details of your day and see how this principle helps you rise above your circumstances.

 Three phrases that rob us of joy are *would have*, *should have*, and *could have*. Avoid using them as much as you can.

On a visit to an army training camp a group of American donors were shown an obstacle course. One of the philanthropists was deeply distressed at the destruction and disarray of the site. He immediately volunteered to have the site cleaned up and paved for the benefit of the soldiers.

The officers showing the group around could barely contain their laughter. The commanding officers explained that the reason for the physical conditions of the site was to develop the physical capacities and fundamental skills and abilities that a soldier must have in combat operations. Negotiating these obstacles successfully develops skills and confidence in the soldiers' mental and physical abilities.

"A PERSON SHOULD ACCUSTOM HIMSELF TO REPEATING, 'ALL THAT HASHEM DOES IS FOR THE GOOD'"

(SHULCHAN ARUCH, ORACH CHAIM 222).

Rabi Akiva's perspective:

Rabban Gamliel, Rabi Elazar ben Azariyah, Rabi Yehoshua and Rabi Akiva went up to Yerushalayim. When they reached Har Hatzofim, they tore their garments in mourning for the destruction of the Beis Hamikdash. When they looked upon the Har Habayis, they saw a fox emerging from the place of the Kodesh Kadashim. The others started weeping, but Rabi Akiva laughed.

They asked him. "Why are you laughing?"

In reply, he asked, "Why are you weeping?"

"This is the place so holy that it is said, 'The stranger that approaches it shall die.' Now foxes roam there freely. Why should we not weep?"

"That is why I laugh," Rabi Akiva explained. "Uria prophesied in the time of the First Beis Hamikdash 'Therefore, because of you, Zion shall be plowed as a field... and the Har Habayis like the high places of a forest.' Later Zechariah prophesized 'Old men and women shall yet sit in the streets of Yerushalayim.' But the Torah makes Zechariah's prophecy dependent on Uriah's.

"As long as Uriah's prophecy had not come about, I feared that Zechariah's prophecy would not either. But now that we see Uriah's prophecy has become a reality, and Har Habayis has become like 'the high places of the forest,' it is certain that Zechariah's prophecy of consolation will be fulfilled as well."

"Akiva, you have consoled us," they told him. "Akiva, you have consoled us!" (Makkos 24b)

LEARN THE ART OF REFRAMING

The *Gemara* relates other similar incidents where Rabi Akiva laughed while his peers wept. He possessed the ability to focus on the positive, even when the situation appeared hopeless. This talent of reframing negative events with positive application can serve as a model for you.

 When you feel negativity springing up inside of you ask yourself, "How would Rabi Akiva have reacted?"

As a young man Rabbi Dovid Refson was involved in anti-missionary work. One of the missionaries accused Rabbi Refson of hitting him, and he spent several weeks in Haifa prison. When he returned to yeshivah, he complained to Reb Elya, "I didn't deserve that!"

Reb Elya jumped up and declared, "A kofer, a heretic! Right here in our yeshivah is someone who doesn't believe that there is a precise cheshbon in Heaven. If it happened," Reb Elya concluded, "you deserved it!" (Rabbi Y.Y. Rubinstein)

Raise your expectations:

Rebbetzin Shifra Nebenzahl was devastated when her husband decided to uproot the family and move to the Old City. She cried and cried. It was soon after the Old City was recaptured and there were no neighbors, no friends for the children, no stores; just cats and ruins. "The first day after we arrived, I opened the shades and looked out and my eyes opened wide. The holiest place in the world was right in front of me! I could take a Tehillim and look out at our holiest site. How privileged I was! I started to cry again asking Hashem forgiveness for having cried the first time."

DON'T UNDERESTIMATE YOUR ABILITIES

CHALLENGE THE INNER VOICE THAT MAKES YOU DOUBT YOUR WORTH

What you think of yourself determines your fate. You are an infinite Divine powerhouse. People tend to fail not because of lack of ability but because of lack of effort and lack of self-confidence. Trying to get by without any effort leaves you feeling terrible. Failing to appreciate our own abilities is like a wealthy man who, having no understanding of his wealth, lives frugally, pinching pennies.

KNOWING WHO AND WHAT YOU ARE IS YOUR GREATEST POWER

You are more powerful than you have been led to believe. You live in a physical body, but you are infinite. That is because you have a Divine soul. You don't have to try to be somebody because you are somebody. Knowing who and what you are is your greatest power. You must challenge that inner voice that makes you doubt our own worth.

Repeat to yourself, "Every day in every way, I am getting better and better" (Rabbi Z. Pliskin). The best investment you will ever make is the investment you make in yourself. It is imperative that you affirm your worthiness over and over again. You must stand tall in the abilities given to you by Hashem.

 Food For Thought

There was once a king who wanted to determine which of his three sons would be the most qualified to rule after him. He gave the first son $1000, the second son $500 and the youngest son only $10. He then told them that the next king would be the one who could fill up a certain room in the palace from floor to ceiling with what they bought.

The first brother bought many wagonloads of straw, which almost filled up the room, but there were some empty spaces here and there. The second one brought many carloads of feathers and replaced the straw with the feathers. He got further than the first brother did but he still didn't reach the top. Finally, the youngest son walked in carrying a small bag. Everybody wondered how he planned on filling up the entire room with the contents of a small bag? To their amazement, he took out some candles and matches. The light of the candles filled up the room! And he became the next king.

YOU CAN LIGHT UP THE WORLD

You can light up the world. For the person who is in a well-balanced emotional state, the possibilities are unlimited. The confidence which comes from within has staying power. This type of self-assurance ensures that you will not be distracted by a need to cater to other's opinions of you.

Inspiration

An elderly chassid once visited the Beis Yisroel to ask for guidance and a brachah. He described his spiritual condition, emphasizing his many shortcomings in all areas of Hashem's service. With a sigh, the chassid concluded, "If I make a spiritual reckoning and take stock of my situation, I realize that I have nothing!"

The Beis Yisroel quickly retorted, "To realize that you have nothing, you don't need to make a spiritual reckoning. You could have concluded that without much thought. But if you make a true calculation, you will realize that you really are abundantly blessed and must strive for more and more!"

AVOID APPROVAL SEEKING

Guidance should always be welcome. Beware, however, of the need for approval and acknowledgement which although always gratifying, turns our focus outwards. Craving outside input is extremely stressful. You may end up investing much more than you bargained for trying to please others. The reality is that different people have different views, so no matter how hard you try there will always be people who find fault with and criticize you.

PREPARE WELL AND DO YOUR BEST

No one will hand you self-confidence; you have to work on it. The best way to achieve that goal is with positive self-talk. Although it is true that success tends to breed confidence, the opposite is also true. Confidence creates the inner environment needed to succeed. Not all people who succeed at life develop good self-esteem. You must decide that you have self-worth and that you are worthy of self-confidence. The good news is that it is true. Prepare well and do your best. Delight in your successes, even if only partial. No more can be asked of you.

"A STRONG DESIRE WITHIN A PERSON GENERATES POWER, ENHANCES THOUGHT PROCESSES, HELPS OVERCOME LAZINESS AND PROPELS A PERSON DOWN THE PATH OF WISDOM" (ALTER OF KELM).

Inspiration

Sometimes Aharon's name appears before Moshe's name, and sometimes the opposite. This is to teach us that they were equal (*Rashi Shemos*, 6: 26).

"How can this be? Moshe was the Master of all the Prophets (See "*Ani Maamin*" 7 of the *Rambam*). The Torah was given through Moshe. So how can we say that Aharon was his equal?

"Since Aharon completely fulfilled the Will of Hashem to the best of his ability, he is considered equal to Moshe. True, Moshe was greater (in capability) and that is why he was given more significant tasks to perform. However, since they both used their individual capability to its fullest potential, they are considered equals" (Rav Moshe Feinstein).

No one could say when Menachem became the black sheep of the family. When he was young, he was a sweet mischievous child. In the early years of school, he did what he was supposed to do. However, by the time he hit sixth grade, he was clearly not interested in school. No one could put their finger on the cause of his downhill slide. It certainly did not help that the only high school that accepted him was rather mediocre.

He soon developed a reputation as a troublemaker,

He soon developed a reputation as a troublemaker, and was thrown out of yeshivah. He was bounced from yeshivah to yeshivah and found himself spending more time on a park bench than at a school desk. His parents tried to win him back with special programs and bribes. They tried shouting at him and reasoning with him; nothing helped.

He was a huge embarrassment to his family. At one point Menachem stopped going to family simchos. Inevitably, he would be asked what he was learning and which yeshivah he was attending and having no answer was an acute embarrassment to him.

When his draft notice arrived, he realized that he would not be eligible for an exemption as a Torah student. His future options passed before his eyes and it wasn't a pretty picture. Fingering the green envelope, he gave serious thought to his future. Who would want to marry him? What would he look like in five years? At that moment, he decided that he would rehabilitate himself. He would cut himself off from his street friends and go back to yeshivah.

Putting his resolves into action was not easy at all. It was challenging to cut his friends out of his life and set out to battle his yetzer hara alone. Despair was his daily companion. Which yeshivah would be ready to open their doors to him?

His supportive family helped him every step of the way. Together they knocked on every door until finally one opened. A middle of the road yeshivah accepted him. He was very grateful and threw himself completely into learning. Slowly he rose up the ladder of success.

For four years he studied very seriously. Finally it

was time for shidduchim. *The girls suggested for him all had issues. Most of them had problems that were frightening. When the* shidduch *did sound like something they could consider, the other side would reject him hands down. His last four years of learning with devotion were swept aside as prospective families looked into the years when his focus was elsewhere. Waves of distress gripped him. Would he ever be permitted to forget the sins of his youth?*

He faced rejection again and again. But instead of resenting the fact that he wasn't being allowed to move on, Menachem said to himself, "Maybe this will help me atone for the lost years of my life."

Two years later when Menachem was truly struggling to maintain his optimism, a wonderful young lady was suggested. Finally – a girl whom he could see himself living with for the rest of his life. A short time later, they were engaged. Menachem's parents hoped that his future would now be smoother than it had been until now.

The couple moved into a small apartment in Yerushalayim. He learned in a kollel and they managed wonderfully. In a short time they had three beautiful children; Menachem and his wife were happy. Time passed and their lives moved along comfortably. Menachem was asked to join the board that ran their apartment building, his sister got married, his father-in-law's business encountered difficulties, he changed kollels, his wife found a new job and so on.

One evening Menachem returned home to find his wife sitting at the table with a newspaper. She had circled an ad in the job-op section. "Looking for a mashgiach *in* a yeshivah for boys who have fallen between the cracks."

"I think this would be perfect for you. You have what it takes to reach out to these boys without pressuring them in any way." Her eyes sparkled as she continued. "I have all the details." Menachem's eyebrows lifted in surprise. His wife smiled coyly, "I already called."

"Are you serious?" Menachem replied astonished. "Why I am not exactly a yeshivah poster boy. Who would hire me for such a responsible position when I have so many failures to my credit?"

"So many failures? What are you talking about?" She was truly astonished. "You have completed the study of Shas in depth. You negotiated compromises on behalf of my father that were lifesavers. You were the only one all the sides felt comfortable with. Who got the customers back if not you? Your expertise has kept this building functioning harmoniously for the last three years."

His wife stopped only to take a deep breath. "You are perfect for the job. Who else could successfully influence these boys? I am certain with the help of Hashem that you will get this job." She circled the telephone number in red and handed the paper to Menachem.

"How will I come up with a letter of recommendation?" He asked. But his wife had left the room. 'She believes in me,' he thought. 'She is actually certain that I am perfect for the job. I've never had anyone believe in me like that.' This was followed by a thought he had never entertained. 'Maybe I am capable of handling this job'.

It took him three days to call. "No we haven't found anyone for the position," the person who answered the phone told him.

"I have no experience," he began, as if apologizing

for calling, but the voice at the other end did not sound disappointed. "Which high school did you study in?" he asked

Menachem stumbled over the words. "That is a bit of a problem..." he stopped, not knowing how to continue. Menachem just wanted to apologize and hang up but the voice surprised him.

"Excellent, it sounds like you just might be the perfect person for us. You will certainly be able to understand our boys."

Menachem got the job and was extremely successful. Soon he was giving shiurim to the boys. He had a way of explaining the Gemara so well that soon he was asked to give a shiur in a more prestigious yeshivah. With the passage of time, Menachem became one of the most prominent Rosh Yeshivahs in our generation. He still works with boys that have fallen between the cracks. His success lies in his ability to convince them how capable and talented they are (Sheifos).

YOU ARE UNIQUE

REJOICE IN FULFILLING YOUR UNIQUE ASSIGNMENT IN THIS WORLD

Every morning you say, "My G-d, the soul that You have placed in me is pure." Your soul is holy, positive and perfectly good. Each human being is unique, and each one of us has a specific mission. You should feel great joy that you were sent to this world with a holy Jewish soul in circumstance which allows you to fulfill your assignment in this world. The whole world was created so that each

"EVERY JEW COMES TO THE WORLD TO FULFILL THEIR DISTINCTIVE MISSION."

(BAAL SHEM TOV)

of us would be able to ignite our soul and enthusiastically fulfill *mitzvos*.

HASHEM HAS A SPECIAL MISSION FOR YOU

Since Hashem sent you to This World as His emissary, there is a unique role that you must play. He has a special mission that only you, with your unique set of talents, can accomplish. You are an individual who responds to the world in your own way. It is never a good idea to expect that you will act or think exactly like other people. Certainly, we have the same approach toward *mitzvos* as other *frum Yidden* and the same goals. Additionally, we want to "blend in" and be part of our *kehillah*. However, within that framework, we will each want to develop ourselves, specializing or concentrating on a certain area; we must forge our own path of specialization. It's something we can think about as we go through life, learning and maturing.

YOU HAVE A SPECIAL SET OF STRENGTHS THAT NOBODY ELSE HAS

It is simpler than you think to be special. Usually it means just being yourself – after all, there is only one you in the entire world. There has never been another person like you and there will never be another person born in this place, to these particular parents, with the unique combination of talents as you have. You have a special set of strengths that nobody else has or ever will have.

A kingdom is yours in your area of uniqueness. If you abandon your assignment and adopt other's roles, you will have lived to no avail. You are the only one who can nurture your unique inclinations to achieve your unique goal (Biale Rebbe).

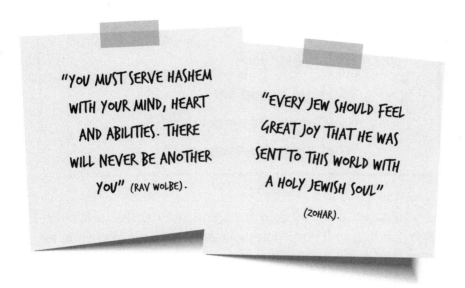

"YOU MUST SERVE HASHEM WITH YOUR MIND, HEART AND ABILITIES. THERE WILL NEVER BE ANOTHER YOU" (RAV WOLBE).

"EVERY JEW SHOULD FEEL GREAT JOY THAT HE WAS SENT TO THIS WORLD WITH A HOLY JEWISH SOUL" (ZOHAR).

YOU ARE A SIGNIFICANT PART OF THE JEWISH PEOPLE

Thinking about these concepts will give you confidence in your worth, so that you can focus on your responsibilities. Of course, as you spread your wings, don't hesitate to consult with those who are successful and experienced, while keeping in mind that results are in Hashem's Hands. Through it all, always remember that you, with your unique personality, are important to your family and friends. You are a significant part of the Jewish people.

FORGE YOUR IDENTITY

It's a fact: If you would do all the things you are capable of doing, you would astound yourself. But what are your capabilities? How can you know how much you can really do? First, you need to forge your Identity.

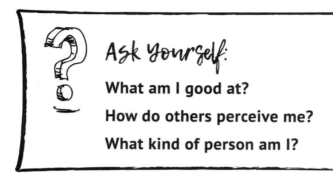

Ask Yourself:

What am I good at?

How do others perceive me?

What kind of person am I?

As you read these questions you may think, "How do I know?" but give it some thought. Make a list of possible answers, and keep working at it. Little by little, you will gain clarity.

When you do, your answers to these questions will be enlightening. By gaining some emotional understanding of yourself you will be able to determine how your characteristics and abilities fit in with the opportunities that are available to you. This understanding is empowering. It will pave the way to good choices and decisions about the future as a valuable member of *Klal Yisroel* and allow you to see yourself as someone who has purpose.

IGNITE THE DIVINE SPARKS WITHIN YOU

Hashem wired us with a need for self-esteem; it readies our

"RAISE YOURSELF UP ABOVE THE CROWD. BRING OUT WHAT MAKES YOU UNIQUE. BECOME A PERSON WHO CAN CHOOSE FOR HIMSELF"

(PIASETZNA REBBE).

neshamah for uplifting motion. The need to feel unique and special is so strong that without it you can feel crushed. When you respect yourself, you ignite the Divine sparks within you. When you truly love yourself and your life, your happiness will overflow. You will have no reason to judge others. You will see only the positive in each person, making it easy for you to care about others and give of yourself to them.

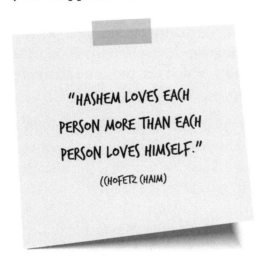

"HASHEM LOVES EACH PERSON MORE THAN EACH PERSON LOVES HIMSELF."

((HOFETZ (HAIM)

A renowned composer was listening to a performance of a complex musical composition. When the concert was over the conductor turned to his companion, shook his head and declared, "Too bad. This piece should have included fourteen violins but one was missing."

The skeptical companion wondered if the composer was right. The next day he contacted the person responsible for the recital. Sure enough, one violinist had called in sick too late for a replacement to be found. The decision was made to proceed without him for it was felt that no one would notice his nonappearance.

The conductor noticed the crucial set of notes that were missing. He was distressed by the fact that the performance was deficient. So too, each of us is an important part of the orchestra of Hashem. If one of us with our unique capabilities is missing, the harmony is incomplete. Each of us must make our own contribution to the Symphony for the Master of the Universe (Rav Yitzchok Zilberstein).

We all play an important role in this symphony. Those with few challenges and those with massive ones each sound a different tone.

Hashem awaits each unique contribution. If a person gives up or does not fully develop himself, he will deprive Hashem of some unique notes which are required to maintain the kingdom of Hashem.

A very special yeshivah boy was diagnosed with a very serious illness. His friends and teachers stormed the heavens with prayers for his recovery but unfortunately, it had been decreed otherwise. After struggling bravely against the illness, he was niftar.

In his last moments when he was floating in and out of consciousness, he made one final request. He said, "Everything I achieved spiritually was due to my teacher in my second year of yeshivah ketanah, Reb Yitzchok. I am therefore requesting that only he eulogize me."

His parents tried to distract him from such morbid thoughts. "You will get better and you will continue to grow spiritually."

He simply smiled a sad smile and said, "My dear parents, I know where I stand and I am joyfully making my preparation to move to the world of truth. I am therefore asking that you promise to do as I have requested."

His parents nodded their head in agreement as hot tears streamed down their faces. Their son smiled happily. He closed his eyes and he did not open them again.

When preparing for their son's funeral they

remembered their son's request. Someone was sent to contact Reb Yitzchok and ask him to speak. The news of his former student's death hit him like a bolt of lightning. He remembered this student well. The images of their interactions flashed before his eyes; his difficulties, his challenges and ultimately his great successes. Reb Yitzchok couldn't believe that his promising young student was no longer alive.

"He asked that I speak at his levaya? Why me?" He couldn't understand why he had been chosen. "Having his current Rosh Yeshivah speak would be so much more appropriate. Who am I to speak in his stead?"

"The niftar's last request was that you speak. He wanted to be eulogized by the teacher who had the greatest impact on his life."

Reb Yitzchok couldn't figure out why his former student had selected him. Why did he attribute his spiritual growth to him?

"You know that it is a mitzvah to honor this type of request." Reb Yitzchok knew that was right. He felt he had no choice and agreed.

When he arrived at the levaya, the boy's father handed him a note. "This was in my son's wallet. He asked us to give it to you."

Reb Yitzchok opened the well-creased piece of paper; suddenly, he understood everything.

It happened just a few years ago. His class was suffering from a major social issue. Too many boys just did not get along with one another. He sat down to consider how he might put an end to the divisiveness. With the help of Hashem he had come up with an idea.

The next day he distributed sheets of paper with the

names of all the boys of the class. Each name was followed by a large empty space. He spoke about the importance of good interpersonal relationships. "Each of us has many positive attributes. Not all of them are so visible; some are rarely used. I want you to take this paper home and record two positive things about each boy in the class."

Reb Yitzchok collected the papers a couple of days later. He took them home and prepared a sheet of paper for each boy with the positive qualities his friends had shared with him.

The results were remarkable. Not only did the social climate improve dramatically, but the boys made extraordinary strides in all areas. Boys who had not been particularly interested in their studies suddenly threw themselves into their learning. Boys who were not intellectually strong were suddenly participating in the classroom give and take.

Reb Yitzchok had attributed the academic upgrading to the improved social environment. Looking at that piece of paper in his hand, he realized that the academic improvement was directly related to the boost of self-esteem that the boys had felt after reading the praise of their peers.

Reb Yitzchok came back to comfort the mourners accompanied by a group of students who were friends of the niftar. Sitting there he told the story of the paper that the niftar's father had given him. The unbelievable happened next. Each of the boys present opened his wallet and removed a folded piece of paper lying deep within. Each paper looked alike but each was a distinctive record of the outstanding attributes of its owner.

Many feelings that had waited a long time to be revealed were shared. By revealing their uniqueness, Reb Yitzchok had propelled these boys to the highest levels of their respective yeshivos (Sheifos).

YOU ARE SPECIAL

BELIEVE IN YOURSELF

Believe in yourself. The earth on which you live, you yourself and everything in your environment is the result of Hashem's personal interest in you. Much painstaking detail went into every aspect of your existence.

> *A group of* mechanchim *asked Rav Hunter what should be the primary emphasis of Torah* chinuch. *He replied, "The primary focus of* chinuch *in today's world is to implant within children the concept of our having been chosen by Hashem, of 'asher bachar banu.'" What he saw as most critical was the need to inculcate the understanding of how special it is to be a Jew* (Rabbi Tzvi Goode, Hamodia, 3 Adar II 5771).

FOCUS ON THE GIFTS YOU HAVE RECEIVED

Every Jew should feel great joy from knowing that he was sent to this world with a holy Jewish soul. Hashem created you in His Image and with His Spirit, which makes you a precious person with a beautiful *neshamah*. Repeat these thoughts to yourself on a regular basis. Don't let the *yetzer hara* convince you otherwise. The *yetzer hara* of our generation is to convince people, *mi ani u'mah ani*-I am a nobody. Your greatest weapon against this falsehood is your ability to focus on the gifts you have received.

AFFIRM YOUR WORTHINESS AGAIN AND AGAIN

Recognizing your great value and potential is an obligation. You must be aware of the inner richness of your being. The refinement of your *neshamah* is a reminder of your glorious spiritual essence. It's imperative that you affirm your worthiness over and over again. This creates an environment geared to success by steering you away from thoughts of failure.

ADVANTAGES OF COMPREHENDING YOUR TRUE WORTH

One of the great things about feeling cherished is that when our heart is full of self-worth the excess spills over into the lives of others in the form of *Ahavas Yisroel*. Nothing is a greater impediment to being on good terms with others than being ill at ease with yourself. Another advantage of comprehending your true worth is that you won't feel compelled to prove it to others. This will free you from a lot of unnecessary pain.

"BEFORE AND AFTER THE GIVING OF THE TORAH HASHEM STRESSED THE LOFTY STATUS OF EVERY SINGLE JEW. WITHOUT AWARENESS OF CHASHIVUS ONE CANNOT SERVE HASHEM" (RAV WOLBE).

"JUST AS A PERSON IS OBLIGATED TO BELIEVE IN HASHEM HE IS REQUIRED TO BELIEVE IN HIMSELF"

(RAV TZADOK HA'KOHEN).

Without reasonable confidence in your own abilities, you cannot be successful or happy. When you recognize your intrinsic worth, you can accept who you are with all your weaknesses - the good and the not so good. You all have shortcomings, but often you feel unable to acknowledge the existence of those faults because you lack the security of recognizing your core value. You must see your essential worth as a given. Then you can handle everything.

This means believing that Hashem loves us, cares for us and is interested in our Torah, *tefillah* and *avodas Hashem*. You must believe that your soul comes from Above and Hashem has pleasure from you and enjoyment when you do His will.

One time the Klausenberger Rebbe was visiting one of his wealthy disciples asking for a donation to a certain hospital. The wealthy disciple told him, "Rebbe, I'll do my best".

Rabbi Halberstam looked at him and paused as if gazing into the past. He then said, "You should know that when you say something like 'I'll do my best', you are committing yourself to a very, very major undertaking."

The Rebbe continued: "Before the holocaust, I had given myself over to Torah study and tefillah – that was my life. I felt I was pushing myself to the very limits of my capabilities and strength and could not possibly do any more whatsoever. But then the war came and all that changed... I was sent to a concentration camp, working 15, 16+ hours a day doing grueling, backbreaking, hard labor with extremely meager food rations for months and years. I pushed and pushed, revealing in myself surprisingly new powers that I did not realize I possessed.

"This taught me that each person possesses superhuman strength which is concealed and can be brought to the surface if he learns to push himself..." (Nitzotos, page 355).

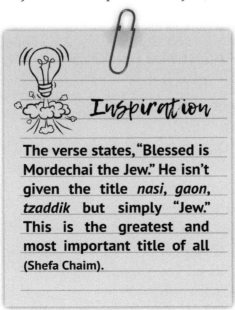

Inspiration

The verse states, "Blessed is Mordechai the Jew." He isn't given the title *nasi*, *gaon*, *tzaddik* but simply "Jew." This is the greatest and most important title of all (Shefa Chaim).

YOU CAN CHANGE THE WORLD

WE ARE HASHEM'S ENVOYS

Each one of us is on a mission from Hashem. We are His extension. Our Job: to spread *malchus* and *Kavod Shamayim.* What does this mean? We must speak and act in ways that personify Him, in all we do, with everyone we

"A PERSON SHOULD LOOK AT HIM/HERSELF AS A TZIR NE'EMAN – A FAITHFUL AMBASSADOR"

(RABEINU YONA).

come in contact with. We must be loyal, dependable, devoted agents of Hashem. We must be conscientious envoys in every way! Everything we do counts and matters! Anyone who has any contact or interaction with us should walk away with a desire to pursue Yiddishkeit.

Mr. Sol Werdiger, CEO of Outerstuff, a company that produces sports apparel, received a phone call from Mr. Joon, the South Korean UN Ambassador asking to meet him for lunch at a Kosher restaurant in Manhattan. Sol agreed to meet with Mr. Joon.

When they met, Mr. Joon got straight to the point. "I have always heard negative stereotypes about Jews and Israel which I took at face value. Then my daughter took an internship working on design in your company. She has only good things to say about how wonderful it is to work at your company."

Mr. Joon continued, "There are four areas which really impressed my daughter.

1) Everyday, at 1:30 p.m., no matter what was going on at the office, all the men including those from neighboring offices, retreated into a room to pray with sincerity and calm. 2) Every Friday the office shuts down early in the afternoon in preparation for your Sabbath and is closed on the Sabbath - this includes all workers no matter which faith or religion they maintain. 3) My daughter observed that each petitioner for charity - and there were many - was treated with respect and left with a check in hand. 4) My daughter was treated with the utmost respect and dignity."

Because of the amazing experience and life changing lessons the company taught his daughter, Mr. Joon took out his checkbook and was ready to write a check returning his daughter's entire earnings! Mr. Werdiger wouldn't consider it. "Your daughter earned her salary and rightfully deserves her pay."

The ambassador was not finished. "As you know, I have voting privileges at the UN. Because of my renewed appreciation of the Jewish people, I abstained from voting on resolutions against Israel on three occasions. At one resolution I was the ninth vote needed to pass the resolution against Israel and because I abstained, it did not pass!" (Rabbi Dovid Saks)

> "EACH PERSON IS REASON ALONE FOR THE CREATION OF THE WORLD, FOR HE HAS THE ABILITY TO INFUSE THE WORLD WITH MEANING"
>
> (RAV CHAIM FRIEDLANDER).

YOU HAVE A CRITICAL MISSION TO FULFILL

> TELL YOURSELF, "I'M IN CONTROL." "I CAN DO THIS." "I CAN MAKE IT HAPPEN." "MY SELF-CONFIDENCE KEEPS GETTING STRONGER AND STRONGER EVERY DAY IN EVERY WAY" (RABBI Z. PLISKIN).

When the Torah was given, one of the accompanying gifts was the ability to bring about change through our actions (Daas Tevunos). There is so much in the world for you to accomplish if you only have the eyes to see the opportunities, the heart to yearn for it and the hands to try it. You were given the opportunity to make improvements to this world! Knowing that you have a critical mission to fulfill helps you to focus.

STEP OUTSIDE YOUR COMFORT ZONE

If you don't pursue what you want you'll never get it. It may seem that everything you want is just outside your comfort zone; a little discomfort is healthy! If you don't step forward you will always remain in the same place. Surround yourself with people and resources to help you get ahead.

> "YOU WERE GRANTED CERTAIN STRENGTHS THAT MUST BE USED TO REALIZE YOUR POTENTIAL. ONCE A PERSON IDENTIFIES THE AREAS IN WHICH HE EXCELS HE CAN THEN ASK, "'AM I USING THESE QUALITIES TO REFINE AND IMPROVE MYSELF AND THE WORLD?'" (RAV DESSLER).

DEVELOP A CLOSE RELATIONSHIP WITH A MENTOR

The Torah is here to help you become the greatest human being ever! *Mitzvos* are designed to break our self-centeredness and force a confrontation with our weaknesses. The fortunate among us receive much support and guidance from parents, family and friends. We are constantly exposed to examples of people whose lives and characters reflect the battle to improve themselves. One of the best investments you can make is to work on developing a close relationship with a teacher or Rav who motivates you on a personal level to be the best you can be (or to bring out the best in you).

HELP FROM ABOVE

Take your idea and bring it to life – make it real. The secret to getting started is to break your overwhelming idea into small manageable parts. Start on the first one and when you are ready, move on to the next. You coax, nurse and entice it to remain alive. When Hashem sees us working to create an environment that will help us grow spiritually, we merit help from Above. The Master of the Universe steps in to sweep aside all opposition.

Inspiration

Yiftach knew how critical self-esteem is. He told the elders of Gilad that if they wanted him to fight on their behalf, they must first appoint him as their leader. Why did he demand that he be crowned as their leader before the battle? After all, he would automatically receive the title if he won! Rav Chaim Shmulevitz explains that Yiftach knew that the self-esteem engendered by the appointment would propel him to victory.

REFUSE TO LISTEN TO THE YETZER HARA

The *yetzer hara* seeks to demoralize man into thinking that his actions have no consequence. You must turn off the *yetzer hara* who tries to persuade you that you are spiritually impoverished and worthless in Hashem's eyes. Refuse to let him "talk" to you; when he begins his persuasive negative-talk, don't let him get an extra word in. Start thinking positive thoughts, review your accomplishments, your plans and sing an uplifting song in your head. You must resist him with all your energy and rather "talk" about the importance of your actions.

When Rav Mordechai Gifter was a boy collecting pictures of gedolim, he purposely left one page blank. When his mother asked him why there was no picture on that page, he explained, "I left a place for my picture. When I get older, I'm going to learn and learn and one day I will be a great Torah scholar and my picture will be on this page."

He never stopped believing in himself and he became the kind of great person with the ability to change the world.

WE ARE THE CHILDREN OF THE KING

BEING A CHILD IS A PERMANENT STATE

"The fact that we are children to Hashem is the foundation of foundations and the essence of essences, to believe that we are children in every

"THE LETDOWN WHICH FOLLOWS FAILURE COMPELS THE PERSON TO UNDERTAKE SELF-IMPROVEMENT"

(RAV CHAIM SHMULEVITZ).

situation.....We are his children in all situations... because a child is always a child, and you can't stop being a child. It's a permanent state" (*Nesivos Shalom al HaTorah*).

THE HAPPINESS OF KNOWING WHO YOU ARE AND WHAT IS EXPECTED OF YOU

When you realize your inborn worth, you awaken your potential for joy. The happiness that ripens from self-esteem derives from knowing who you are and what is expected of you. It comes with the feeling of knowing with a certainty that you are moving toward your goal. When you consider the grandeur and splendor Hashem has granted us you are compelled to realize that sadness is unbecoming to our royal status. The entire Jewish people are called *bnei melachim*-princes.

HASHEM SHOWERS HIS CHILD WITH BLESSING

Imagine a king who wished to punish his disobedient son. Whenever he summons him to discipline him, however, the prince shows such pleasure at being with his father that the king cannot bring himself to administer the punishment. When we show happiness at being Hashem's child, Hashem reacts by showering us with blessing.

"A PERSON WHO PERCEIVES HIMSELF IN ALL OF HIS GRANDEUR AND SPLENDOR WOULD HARDLY BE CAPABLE OF ACTING IN A MANNER NOT BEFITTING THE ROYAL STATION TO WHICH HE HAS BEEN ELEVATED" (ALTER OF SLOBODKA).

ALWAYS ACT AS IF YOU ARE WEARING AN INVISIBLE CROWN

As needed, keep repeating to yourself, "I am a child of Hashem." "I love Hashem and Hashem loves me." Always act as if you are you wearing an invisible crown. You can then say to yourself, "A person of my stature, a descendant of great people, with so many achievements to my credit, can't possibly consider transgressing" or better perhaps "behaving any less than the best".

 Food For Thought

Rabbi Manis Mandel would often tell his students, "Low key, low key, low key. It doesn't matter that the world is not this way. You are not 'the world.' You are the daughters of Hashem" (Rabbi Manis Mandel page 211).

Being a daughter of Hashem obliges us to act accordingly.

INTERNALIZE YOUR IMPORTANCE

When things appear to be holding us back, it is merely a passing phase, not permanent. Most often we fail because we were distracted by a tornado of desire or because of some trauma, and we don't realize that it will pass with time. The most important question is what one does after the storm. One who has internalized that he is important will dust himself off and begin again, no matter what.

Inspiration

Hashem takes pride in each and every Jew - even sinners. If people who go off the derech would only understand this principle, realizing that they can always start over again no matter what, they would never fall far. Instead, they would fight for every drop of holiness they could grab in this harsh world of constant temptation and challenge (Rav Nosson of Breslav).

Rav Tzadok develops this same idea another way. "How sad for the person who does not realize that it is never too late. He is cheated out of all the potential good he could achieve. If he only understood that what he does is important, and that every bad can be transformed into good, he could accomplish so much" (Pri Tzaddik).

ACT ON YOUR INSPIRATION

When you feel inspired, it is important to act immediately. This inspiration may be a gift from Hashem. Treat it with respect and act upon it as soon as you can.

When the Tchebiner Rov heard that one of his students had abandoned all religious observance, the rov sent a messenger asking that he come to speak with him. Although the boy had already strayed quite a distance he still held the rov in high esteem, so he came.

The rov looked at him with loving eyes, his heart overflowing with pity for his former student. He wanted to save him. But how? He knew that he wouldn't accomplish a thing with rebuke. After a short tefillah to the Ribono Shel Olam he turned to the boy and said, "Please, listen to me Mendel. You know very well that you are not just any Mendel. You are special. You are a descendant of royalty. You are a link in the chain of the dynasty of Ziditchov. That means you are a prince. This is a tremendous privilege...but it also obligates you. Did you know that in Ziditchov they have a custom not to say Tachanun during Shacharis each Friday? This custom, instituted by the holy Rav Hershele of Ziditchov, has been maintained by his children and grandchildren. Since you are their descendant, you must hold on to this custom with pride."

Mendel smiled. He liked the idea. He had assumed that the rov would give him a whole lot of directives, which he was ready to adamantly refuse. But he had no reason to refuse to keep such a custom. He readily swore that he would keep this directive.

Mendel slipped off the straight path down a slippery slope which led him to the lowest depths. But he never forgot his promise to the rov. Every Erev Shabbos he would say to himself, "Tachanun? No, it's Friday. Today we don't say Tachanun no matter what."

Time passed. One Friday, Mendel said to himself, "What I am doing makes no sense. I am upholding a custom not to say Tachanun, but I don't even daven so not saying Tachanun is of no relevance. Only if I daven will it be clear that I am omitting Tachanun because I *am a descendant of the Ziditchover Rebbe." That Friday, Mendel davened, and from that week he never missed Friday morning Shacharis.*

At a later date, it occurred to him that not davening the rest of the week made it impossible for anyone to know that he left out Tachanun on Fridays only. So he decided to daven every day. This went on a for a while until one day it occurred to him that it was really incongruous to be davening every day to the Ribono Shel Olam while being mechallel Shabbos. So, he became shomer Shabbos.

Slowly, but surely, he kept moving upwards, higher and higher, until his holy soul was able to completely shake off the foreign influence of impurity that got hold of it to begin with. Mendel returned to being a full-fledged Jew. He married and built a beautiful Torah home. It started with the realization that he was special, that he was a prince of royal lineage (Gilyon Shaarei Eison as cited by Rabbi Yitzchok Tzvi Schwartz, Yated 4th of Sivan 5776).

YOUR POWER IS INFINITE

WE HAVE BEEN GIVEN AN IMPORTANT MISSION

Hashem has given each of us a precious *neshamah* with our own special set of strengths that no one else has or will have. He has given us an important mission. It is like being handed the crown of the king to guard. One should feel overwhelmed by Hashem's love and trust (Rav Aharon Kotler).

YOU CAN SUCCEED

The people who get far in life generally are the ones who think they can succeed. You are here to offer the world the talents and skills that you have. Using your creative power generates joy, liveliness, generosity and compassion. It makes us indifferent to fighting and the accumulation of objects and money. How much more you can accomplish if you live a life that is passionate and creative than one that is tied to acquiring things.

 Food For Thought

Rav Shlomo Heiman once asked Rav Manis Mandel, "How are things going?"

Rabbi Mandel replied, "Baruch Hashem."

"Are you perhaps satisfied with a little?"

He was concerned that Rabbi Mandel should never be satisfied with the status quo but always strive for greater heights (Rabbi Manis Mandel page 69).

GATEWAY TO SUCCESS

The first gateway into the service of Hashem is knowing your self-worth and recognizing your strengths. Think, or even better yet say, "I am a great and important person who possesses many good and exalted traits, the descendant of greatness and royalty. How can I possibly commit an evil deed and sin against my G-d and my forefathers?"

If *chas v'shalom*, we do not recognize our

> "THERE IS A CRUSHING FORCE BUILT INTO HUMAN NATURE, WHICH TRIES TO TOPPLE A PERSON TO THE GROUND BY MAKING ONE FEEL WORTHLESS"
>
> (RAV SIMCHA ZISEL OF KELM).

greatness and the greatness of our forefathers, it is easy to follow immoral paths, and then get sucked into seeking to indulge our base urges relentlessly (Rabbeinu Yonah).

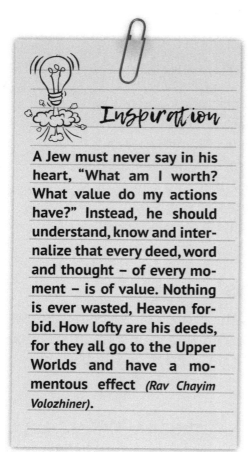

Inspiration

A Jew must never say in his heart, "What am I worth? What value do my actions have?" Instead, he should understand, know and internalize that every deed, word and thought – of every moment – is of value. Nothing is ever wasted, Heaven forbid. How lofty are his deeds, for they all go to the Upper Worlds and have a momentous effect *(Rav Chayim Volozhiner)*.

Andrew Carnegie hired Napoleon Hill to make a long study of success. One of the most powerful forecasters of success was the power of belief. Mr. Hill demonstrated that it was not the most gifted or talented people who succeeded but the ones who believed in themselves and worked hard.

HASHEM GUIDES YOU TO SUCCESS

There is nothing more fragile than a snow flake but consider what it can do when it bonds with others. Think of all the times you felt certain that you wouldn't be able to do something, yet in the end, you succeeded. You have surmounted so many obstacles you believed could not be vanquished but Hashem sent messengers to help you. You have made it through every single challenge you've faced and each one of them helped you become the person you are today.

"WHEN SOMETHING NEEDED TO BE DONE, I NEVER GAVE ANY THOUGHT AS TO WHETHER I WAS ABLE TO DO IT OR NOT. IF I WAS CERTAIN THAT IT WAS NECESSARY, I WOULD FIND A WAY TO GET IT DONE"

(ALTER OF NOVARDOK).

During the Holocaust, Rav Yaakov Galinsky was imprisoned by the Soviets and sent to Siberia. A certain prisoner, a Lithuanian, stuck out among the others, in more ways than one; this man stood very tall and straight as a ramrod. In addition, it appeared that he was being singled out for the most grueling and humiliating labor.

All day long, this Lithuanian P.O.W. fulfilled his tasks without uttering a word. At night, he collapsed on the floor. He had a small rucksack that he guarded carefully. No one was allowed to look inside. When he slept, he used it as a pillow. In the morning, he hid it. He retrieved it only when it was again time to go to sleep.

The other prisoners were very curious to know what was in that sack, but its owner was a man of few words and not about to reveal his secret.

One night, Rav Galinsky could not sleep. Suddenly, a noise form the corner of the room attracted his attention. Straining his eyes in the dark, he couldn't believe what he *was seeing. The tall prisoner was reaching into his sack with great care and extracting a complete army uniform. Looking around to assure himself that everyone was sound asleep, the man pulled on the uniform, right over his prison garb. Rising to his full height, he smartly executed a few commanding maneuvers. He then quickly removed the uniform, replaced it carefully into his sack, and went to sleep.*

Walking to their labor site the next day, Rav Galinsky asked the man, "Why do you slip on an army uniform in the middle of the night?"

The man turned white, then red. Making sure that they weren't overheard, Rav Galinsky managed to persuade him that he could be trusted. Then the man confided, "I used to be a top commander in the Lithuanian army. As you see, the Russians are sparing no effort to break my spirit. I get the most grueling tasks and the most mortifying assignments, all in an attempt to degrade me and destroy my spirit.

"I, on the other hand, refuse to allow a total breakdown. So every night, I take out my army uniform. I want to remember the real me. I don't want to forget that I am really a successful commander, capable of executing the most demanding tasks."

Rav Galinsky was always quick to add that eventually this commander was sent home in a prisoner exchange and presumably restored to his former glory. "What I learned from that accursed Lithuanian was that in every situation, a person must remember who he is. In this way, each *Yid* must recall that he is the son of the King of Kings–*Hashem.*

REMEMBER YOUR TRIUMPHS

SAVOR YOUR SUCCESSES

Review everything that went right during the course of the day. Savor the success of what you have accomplished. Consider how you got dressed and out of the house without any glitches, you wished your mother a great day, you made it to school on time, all your homework was done, you took a moment to cheer up a friend. Spend a few minutes each day thinking about everything that went right. Focusing on the positive things in your life will lead to continued happiness.

Recall various events of the last year that made you very happy. What was it that made you feel good in a lasting way? Did you ever experience a sense of awe? Did it come from a remarkable achievement or from a connection you felt to someone else? Did you meet a challenge with success? Savor these events and commit yourself to traveling that route again in the future.

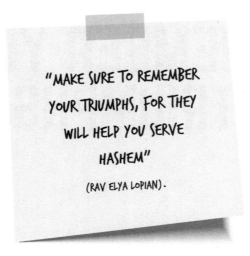

"MAKE SURE TO REMEMBER YOUR TRIUMPHS, FOR THEY WILL HELP YOU SERVE HASHEM"

(RAV ELYA LOPIAN).

When Dovid Ha'melech was still a young shepherd, he killed a fierce lion and a wild bear that attacked his sheep. Dovid knew that Hashem had saved him. He made a jacket from the lion's skin, which he wore to remind himself of his miraculous triumph and its portent for the future.

When he came forward to offer his services to kill Golias, he declared, "Hashem, who saved me from the lion and the bear, will save me from the Pelishtim" (Shmuel I 17:37).

SEE YOURSELF GETTING BETTER AND BETTER IN THE FUTURE

Enjoying your success will not make you proud. Everyone

has both successes and failures. Acknowledge what you do well and what you need to improve in. True, nothing is perfect, so as you focus on past successes see yourself getting better and better in the future.

YOU ARE YOUR OWN BEST FRIEND

LIVE YOUR DREAMS WITH GREATER CONFIDENCE

Your life experiences have increased your wisdom and understanding. Life becomes easier when you realize you have the ability to fall back on the skills you have mastered. Of course you will constantly need to consult with your seniors but it becomes possible to try living your dreams with greater confidence. You won't endlessly seek out validation from the wrong sources.

IF YOU WOULDN'T SAY IT TO YOUR GOOD FRIEND DON'T SAY IT TO YOURSELF

When you believe in yourself your thoughts will

eventually manifest themselves in outward, physical action, and gradually transform your actual reality. The relationship you have with yourself sets the standard for your relationship with others. When your mood is low, take the time to list the many great things about you. Noticing the negative? If you wouldn't say it to your good friend then don't say it to yourself. If you have nothing nice to say about yourself don't say anything. Remember you must live with yourself as long as Hashem grants you life. Who enjoys living with someone who is always critical?

> "ELOKEINU VE'ELOKEI AVOSEINU"
> THE USE OF THE WORD ELOKEINU (YOUR
> G-D) TEACHES THAT YOU MUST WORK
> ON YOUR OWN RELATIONSHIP WITH
> HASHEM AND NOT RELY ON YOUR
> PARENTS AND ZEIDES AND BABAS
> (BAAL SHEM TOV).

REACHING OUT TO OTHERS

Remember what Hillel said, "If I am not for myself, who will be for me?" Read about great people. Learn to think great thoughts. Find a *mashpiah* with whom you feel comfortable sharing what's on your mind and in your heart.

REACTING TO CRITICISM

What if someone criticizes your taste in clothing, your drawing or your actions? If the comments are legitimate and you consider the subject important, take action to correct what you have done, or to improve. If the comments have little value, or the subject is of no importance, say to yourself, "I chose the style, color etc. that I like. Others don't have to like it. As long as it is modest, within the norm, and not eye-catching, I can choose what I like."

EVERYONE HAS DIFFERENT WAYS OF LOOKING AT THINGS

If someone asks for your opinion or advice, and then doesn't accept it, don't take this personally. They thought highly enough of you to ask; there can be many reasons why their final decision did not reflect your input. Remind yourself that everyone has a different way of looking at things. Disagreeing with your opinion isn't necessarily a reflection on you. Judge yourself only in relation to yourself – according to your struggles and efforts. Then do the best you can while striving to be realistic.

"THE GOAL OF THE MITZVAH OF LIGHTING THE MENORAH IS NOT THE ACT OF LIGHTING THE CANDLES BUT RATHER A PROCESS OF ENSURING THAT THE CANDLES BURN. THE OBJECTIVE IS TO MAKE SURE THAT THEY ARE BURNING ON THEIR OWN" (RAV YOSEF YITZCHOK OF LUBAVITCH).

Reb Yissachar Ber of Radoshitz once met an old peas-
ant who had known him when he was a boy. The gentile
was not aware that he had become a well-known Rebbe.

"Berele!" he called out when he saw the Rebbe.

The Rebbe greeted the old man pleasantly. "And
what's new with you?" he asked.

The old man shrugged and replied, "Well, Berele,
what should I tell you? What you don't get by your own
work, you don't have."

From that time on, whenever the Radoshitzer Rebbe
spoke about the proper way to conduct one's life, he
always added, "And as the old man of Oleshnye said,
'What you don't get by your own work, you don't have'"
(Mipi Chassidim).

DON'T GET DISCOURAGED

YOUR IMPERFECTIONS ARE NOT WHO YOU REALLY ARE

Every small gesture of reaching out to Hashem is a huge accomplishment. Don't let your deficiencies faze you or slow you down. Your imperfections are not who you really are; they are outer garments that can be shed. When bad voices speak up, drown them out with good voices.

PERSEVERANCE IS MORE IMPORTANT THAN TALENT

Hashem gave you the exact deficiencies that you need to have to bring out your potential. Perseverance is more important than talent. *Chazal* inform us that successful living requires *mesiras nefesh*. It means forcing yourself onward even as the effort becomes really difficult. When you are discouraged, it is usually because you are trying to do things on your own. Boost your optimism by remembering that Hashem is in control.

> *"IT IS VITAL TO FIGHT DEPRESSION AS ONE WOULD FIGHT THE GREATEST ENEMY AND TO RUN FROM IT AS ONE WOULD RUN FROM DEATH ITSELF"* (SEFER HA'MIDDOS).

WAIT IT OUT

Everyone can have a streak of good days and then suddenly you feel like a storm is brewing inside. You are not responsible for actions or lack of actions that are beyond your control. It helps to try to understand what is churning inside. There is a lot to figure out and the hormones inside don't help things get any clearer. Sometimes the best thing you can do is to wait it out.

PRACTICE BEING BRAVE

You're fine so long as things are progressing smoothly but if there is a problem you get extremely frustrated. On some days, nothing seems to be going right. It could be disappointment over a grade or not being chosen by a friend or a teacher for a special activity. There are times when there is tension at home. These depressing days allow you to practice being brave.

TAKE CONTROL OF YOUR THOUGHTS

Sadness is often the result of thoughts such as: "these things should not be happening to a person like me," (Reb Pinchas of Koretz) or "I must have it and it is mine by right" (Reb Aharon Ha'gadol of Karlin).

I often repeat to myself the words of the Gerrer Rebbe, *"Geshenisht sennen bashert ober agmas nefesh macht man alien-* You can't control what happens to you but you can control your reaction." Indeed, no one can make you feel bad unless you let him or her.

"A DISCONTENTED, DISSATISFIED HEART WEAKENS THE LIMBS AND PARALYZES ACTIVITY, WHILE GOOD CHEER BRIGHTENS THE OUTLOOK AND STRAIGHTENS THE BODY"

(RAV S.R. HIRSCH).

NO-ONE'S LIFE IS SMOOTH SAILING

You know that you can't expect life to be trouble free. Yet glitches can totally overwhelm you, as if they were very unexpected. The same goes for your expectations of other people. You expect them to behave in certain ways and when they don't you get upset. You expect certain reactions from people and when you don't get them you are disappointed. One would believe, watching people's reactions to minor problems that they assume their lives are smooth sailing. Why is that so when you know that there is no such thing?

> Rav Moshe Schneider was asked by one of his students for a blessing of a life without problems.
>
> The Rosh Yeshivah replied, "That's not a brachah, there's no such thing as a life without any problems! You should ask for a blessing that you'll be able to overcome the challenges that Hashem sends you in life."

DO WHAT IT TAKES TO HELP YOU FEEL JOYOUS

When you remind yourself that life is not trouble free it makes it easier to deal with the troubles. Sadness must be avoided at all costs. It leads to laziness and procrastination. If possible, express your feelings instead of having them burrow into your heart affecting your behavior. Do what it takes to help you feel joyous.

> "A PERSON MUST FORCIBLY GRASP AND TAKE HOLD OF HIS SORROW, AND CHANGE IT INTO JOY"
>
> (LIKUTEI MOHARAN).

When the Saraf of Strelisk passed away, a large group of his chassidim went to Ruzhin. They appointed one of their group to enter the inner sanctum and ask the Rebbe for spiritual guidance for all of them.

When he was ushered into the Rebbe's presence, the chassid was so overcome with fear that he nearly retreated. Before he turned away, however, the Ruzhiner asked him what he wanted.

Trembling, the chassid presented the request of his friends. The Ruzhiner replied, "Tell them that they should always be joyous. Even if the joy is artificial, it will eventually become authentic" (Le'yoatzei Shalom Simcha).

OBSTACLES CAN BECOME TOOLS FOR SUCCESS

The most notable success stories revolve around those who encountered heartbreaking obstacles before they triumphed. They absolutely refused to become discouraged by their setbacks. They picked up the pieces and continued. Actually, in many cases, the obstacles became their tools for success.

 Food For Thought

IBM turned down Betty Nesmith Graham - the inventor of Liquid Paper - when she offered to sell her invention to them. For 17 years she continued to sell her product from her garage. In 1979 Gillette bought Liquid Paper for $47.5 million plus royalties!

A king owned a diamond of such size and flawless beauty that it had no equal. One day, the diamond was accidentally scratched. The king summoned the most skilled diamond cutters and offered them a great reward to remove the imperfection from his treasured jewel, but none could do so. The king was deeply distressed.

Finally, a gifted jeweler came to the king and promised to make the diamond even more beautiful than it had been before the accident. The king, impressed by his confidence, entrusted the stone to his care. With superb artistry, the jeweler carefully engraved a lovely rosebud around the imperfection, using the scratch to form the stem.

We can control our reaction to our challenges. The wise person zeroes in on the positive. This may take practice. Keep asking yourself, "How can I view this situation in a different, more positive manner?"

"IF YOU ARE ALWAYS JOYOUS, HASHEM WILL HELP YOU IN ALL CIRCUMSTANCES AND IF NOT, WHO KNOWS WHAT WILL BE YOUR END!"

(RAV MOSHE OF KOBRIN)

THE POWER OF JOY

POSITIVE THOUGHTS PROMOTE FAVORABLE CIRCUMSTANCES

Hashem leads a person in the way he wishes to go. Most people are as happy as they wish to be. If you have concluded that joy is beyond your reach, you can always *daven* for *simcha* (See *Tehillim* 86:4). Man's joy draws

"IF ONE STANDS WITH A SHINING FACE BELOW, HE IS ILLUMINATED FROM ABOVE. IF HE STANDS SADLY BELOW, JUDGMENT IS METED OUT TO HIM" (ZOHAR).

down additional joy from above. Positive thoughts promote favorable circumstances and further opportunities for happiness. A person who has achieved a joyous perspective can expect more Divine assistance than he previously merited.

HAPPINESS MAKES YOU A RECEPTACLE OF BLESSING

Happiness turns a person into a receptacle that is capable of receiving blessing. Yona prophesized for the first time after being inspired by the joyous celebration at the *Simchas Beis Ha'shoeiva* (*Yalkut Shimoni* based on *Yerushalmi Sukkah*). When Elisha wished to prophesize, he asked musicians to be brought. The music they played had the power to awaken joy and prophecy (Melachim II 3:15).

WITH JOY YOU CAN REACH YOUR GOALS

Joy gives us increased energy and enthusiasm, enabling us to rise above all personal limitations and weakness. With joy, you're not afraid to start that new venture. You have ambition, buoyancy - you're alive! You can achieve goals that otherwise may seem too difficult to attempt.

"A PERSON SHOULD LABOR TO ACQUIRE THE MIDDAH OF JOY, FOR EVEN THE LOWEST LEVEL OF JOY ORIGINATES IN HOLINESS"

(REB AHARON HA'GADOL OF KARLIN).

JOY IS LIKE SUNSHINE

When you are happy, you are able to share contentment and joy, making you beloved by others.

Upbeat expressions and encouraging words bring sunshine into every room. A Torah Jew with a smile on her face is a walking *kiddush Hashem*.

JOY HEALS

Joyousness heals, as King Shlomo wrote: "A happy heart is as healing as medicine" (*Mishlei* 17:22). Use music or dance to pick yourself up. If you enjoy drawing or writing, use your pencil to bring yourself to a happier place. These are all good ways of expressing your sadness and getting rid of your bad feelings.

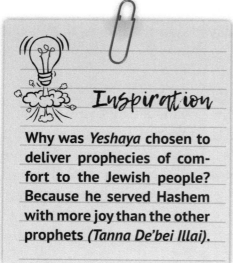

Inspiration

Why was *Yeshaya* chosen to deliver prophecies of comfort to the Jewish people? Because he served Hashem with more joy than the other prophets *(Tanna De'bei Illai)*.

Laugh at your mistakes as you learn from them. Joke over your troubles as you overcome them. When you've learned to laugh at the things that should be laughed at and not to laugh at those that shouldn't, you've acquired wisdom and understanding.

A couple living in Williamsburg had an only child who was seriously ill. A friend suggested that they see the Satmar Rebbe for a blessing. Although they were not Satmar chassidim, the desperate parents ran to the Rebbe's house in the hope that he would be able to help their daughter.

At the meeting, the Rebbe gently asked the man where he was from. Uninterested in small talk, the father quickly replied that he was descended from Sanzer chassidim, and his father had been a chazzan. He then tried to turn the conversation back to his child.

The Rebbe would not be sidetracked. He asked if he remembered any Sanzer niggunim that his father had sung, and insisted that he sing one on the spot. Unable to refuse the Rebbe, the man began to sing one of his father's favorites.

To the man's own surprise, as he sang the words of Tehillim, waves of tranquility began flowing through him. The Rebbe had achieved his goal of raising the father above the pain to an elated trusting level that would drive away his fear and give him the strength to believe that a cure was a real possibility.

Building on the power of this newfound euphoric trust, the Rebbe then blessed their daughter, who speedily recovered (Moshian Shel Yisroel).

CONNECT TO YOUR FAMILY

DON'T MISS OUT ON FAMILY

Sometimes when you are going too fast, you miss out on so much. There is a lot to be gained by slowing down and thoughtfully looking around especially at your extended family that you interact with all the time. More than anything else people yearn to communicate with those they are close to.

WHY IS KIBBUD AV VA'EM NEGLECTED

Every mitzvah has its mazel (Peleh Yoetz). People spend a lot of money on *segulos* that are not even mitzvos but neglect *mitzvos mi'd'Oraisa*. Consider *kibbud av va'em*. It is easier to be kind to your friends than it is to be kind at home. There is more payback and recognition in return for being nice to outsiders. When you help a stranger, you are acknowledged and appreciated.

When helping a family member, it is quite possible that you will not even receive a thank you because it is expected. It is difficult to help when there is little or no appreciation. Often you have to deal with complaints for not doing more.

 Food For Thought

There was a community in the United States by the name of Roseto where heart disease was unknown amongst their citizens who were under the age of 65. This was years before medications to combat heart disease were available. Interestingly, their diets were rich in foods that promoted heart disease. They didn't exercise much. When relatives living elsewhere were tracked down they had as much heart disease as the general population, so it wasn't hardy genes. People in neighboring communities in Pennsylvania had heart disease at normal levels so there was nothing in the environment that promoted good heart health.

So what was it? The doctor studying this phenomenon decided that it had to be the town itself. After much interviewing, they discovered that the Rosetans were like one big family, visiting one another, stopping to chat on the street and cooking for one another often. In many homes, three generations lived under one roof and grandparents commanded a great deal of respect. They were religious people who prayed regularly and volunteered their time to help others.

SUGGESTIONS

Sadly, bad feelings you have acquired at school can surface at home in the form of anger and jealousy. Make up for these trying times with acts of kindness. Tell your parents how much you appreciate them. Help in the house without being asked. Call if you are delayed. Sit down and schmooze with your mother and father, and later, with your younger sister. Throughout your busy day, as you hear interesting stories or *halachos*, think: is this something I can share with members of my family? Walk into your home prepared!

 Food For Thought

The *Meshech Chochmah* tells us that the *Beis Hamikdash* was built on Binyamin's portion because he was the only one among the brothers who didn't cause his father distress and sorrow, as he wasn't present during the sale of Yosef; neither did he participate.

THE JOY OF GRANDPARENTS

Another valuable goldmine worth cultivating is your relationship with your grandparents. Many of my generation grew up without grandparents; we lost out on the benefits from the unique perspectives - born of wisdom and experience - that grandparents can offer. Grandparents are important role models. As family historians, they can help you find your identity in a larger context. Turn to them often; you will both gain so much.

The Kibbud Em of the Gerrer Rebbe.

Once the Gerrer Rebbe R'Avrohom Mordechai Alter was traveling from Ger to Biala; he learned almost non-stop throughout the trip, as usual. A young man observing the Rebbe noticed him putting his Gemara down late at night and reaching for a sandwich. He went to wash his hands and returned to his seat to eat.

His observer was surprised. All day long the young scholar seemed oblivious to any thought of food but now he was eating with a very happy expression on his face, Unable to control his curiosity, he asked R'Avraham Mordechai to explain.

"Simple," replied the future Rebbe. "I really am not hungry. However, as I was leaving Ger, my mother handed me the sandwich and begged me to make sure to eat it for supper tonight. When I glanced at my watch, I realized that I had not yet fulfilled my mother's request. Now I am doing this mitzvah, should I not be delighted?"

How not to behave.

Reb Shlomo Zalman Auerbach once saw a father carrying tables and chairs on Shabbos (apparently preparing for a family simcha) while his older sons were standing outside, wearing their talleisim and talking. Reb Shlomo Zalman couldn't understand why they weren't helping their father and he asked them to explain. They told him, "We don't carry on Shabbos." There was an eiruv in Yerushalayim but they followed the stringent opinion that prohibited carrying.

For the next three days, Reb Shlomo Zalman didn't give his shiur in yeshiva. He simply couldn't. He didn't have peace of mind. He was so greatly disturbed by what he had witnessed. To actually see young men callously allowing their father to work, hard and refraining from doing the task instead was more than he could bear? It hurt him to witness someone being machmir on a chumra instead of fulfilling a d'Oraisa -Favoring a rabbinic stringency over a Torah prohibition.

 Are you a respectful daughter? Take this self-evaluation and decide for yourself.

- Do you address and speak to your parents respectfully? (This would include responding promptly when you are called and not interrupting them.)

- Do you avoid sitting in your father or mother's place?

- Do you stand up when your parents enter the room?

- Do you make sure not to cause your parents anguish or anger? (This would include not fighting with siblings and not doing anything that would embarrass your parents.)

- Are you careful never to waken your parents?

- Do you make sure not to keep a parent waiting?

- Do you avoid asking them to do something on your behalf and when you need their help do you ask them respectfully?

- Are you careful not to pressure your parents in any way?

- Are you careful not to contradict your parents while also not validating their statements? (As if they needed your reinforcement.)

ANSWER KEY

7-9 yes's - You are a devoted daughter

4-6 yes's - You are getting there

< 4 yes's - Still a way to go

THE JOY OF HELPING OTHERS

BE SOMEBODY WHO MAKES EVERYBODY FEEL LIKE A SOMEBODY

If you dream of making a difference in the world, begin at home and in school. Be somebody who makes everybody feel like a somebody. Everyone wants to be respected for who they are. Try to understand their point of view, or just accept it. Master the art of *vatranus*. *Vatranus* means giving up one's own comfort for the benefit of another. It means putting your friend's feelings on the front burner of your consciousness.

When Reb Chaim Kreisworth was a bachur, he had to walk two hours from his sleeping quarters to yeshivah.

He looked forward to the time when he would be able to get a bed in the yeshivah and not need to spend so much time and effort going back and forth.

Finally that day arrived. A bed was available and it was Reb Chaim's turn to get it. Reb Chaim was overjoyed. Before he actually moved in, another bachur approached him and asked, "I heard that you are getting the bed in the yeshivah, is that correct?" He didn't come out and say it outright but it was clear to Reb Chaim that the bachur was implying, "Why are you getting this bed and not me?"

Reb Chaim knew that this bochur was depressed and having a bed in yeshivah would boost his spirits. Reb Chaim allowed the bachur to take the bed and he continued walking back and forth to yeshiva.

Not long after, the Nazis yemach shemam rounded up the yeshivah boys to kill them. One by one they were led in front of an open window where they were shot and thrown out into the street. Reb Chaim turned to the wall and beseeched Hashem to spare his life with the following tefillah, "Only You know how hard it was for me to give away my bed. In this merit please save me."

When his turn came he pleaded with the Nazi to save his life. The wicked Nazi had pity on him. He shot at the wall instead of on Reb Chaim. He fell to the ground pretending he was shot. When he was thrown out the window, he ran for his life. He was convinced that he survived in the merit of his vatranus (Rav Elimelech Biederman).

REVEAL THE GOOD THAT LIES WITHIN OTHERS

A prominent *chassidish mashpiah*, Rav Gad'l Eisner,

would say that encouragement can revolutionize a person. Being nice to your friends is not simply a matter of politeness. It's an effort to reveal the image of Hashem within them (and within ourselves).

It's your job to take every person you meet and reveal the good that lies within him (Rav Wolbe). From the moment you were born, others cared for you constantly. You were washed, dressed, diapered, fed and nurtured. Now it's time to even the score by helping others, and there is much joy to be found in returning the favors.

TRY TO BE A GOOD LISTENER

Speak kindly and compassionately to others. Do not speak too much about yourself. People desperately need listeners. Try to be a good listener. Listen with your ears, eyes and heart. Maintaining eye contact is important. Try to pick up on what they are not saying and with sensitively, give some uplifting feedback. Warning: do not probe.

THE DELIGHTFUL RESULTS OF HELPING OTHERS

Compassion connects you to others. It is very empowering to step out of the box of your daily concerns and contribute to the larger community. Even doing simple things can make a huge difference in a marvelous chain reaction of joy. Good deeds help make people happy. When you make someone happy, it enhances your self-esteem and people try to make you happy in return. Beyond the sheer joy that comes with helping others, and beyond the lift in your self-esteem, delight in the knowledge that you will be rewarded beyond measure for your kindness.

A few months before Rav Manis Mandel was niftar, he remarked, "I never had a bad day in my life." This was an astounding statement, considering the many challenging periods he had experienced. The secret of his attitude was his constant focus on the needs of others, while ignoring his own hardships.

Ideas For Helping Others

- **Don't talk so much today, try listening more.**
- **Give three compliments today.**
- **Write a Thank-you note to someone.**

You have so much to gain by taking the time to plan to do good deeds. Resolve to help others with no strings attached. For example, ask someone you care about how they are doing and take the time to listen to their answer. Try to be sensitive to how your actions affect people around you. Truly listening when someone speaks becomes easy when you set your mind to do it, and it is such a worthwhile way to help others.

The Chofetz Chaim on helping others.

A community near Radin asked a bachur

"A SOUL CAN BE BROUGHT DOWN TO THIS WORLD FOR SEVENTY OR EIGHTY YEARS IN ORDER TO PERFORM A SINGLE FAVOR FOR A FELLOW JEW, MATERIALLY OR SPIRITUALLY"

(BAAL SHEM TOV).

from the Chofetz Chaim's yeshivah to join them for Rosh Hashanah. They wanted someone of his caliber to inspire their community to do teshuvah *on these holy days.*

The bachur *refused. He wanted to spend his Rosh Hashanah with the Chofetz Chaim.*

The Chofetz Chaim responded by telling the bachur, *A* mentch leibt nisht far zich—*"man doesn't live for himself." The* bachur *understood and went to the neighboring community for Rosh Hashanah.*

Rav Chaim Ozer on helping others.

Rav Chaim Ozer Grodzinsky said, "When I was young, I thought that the greatest accomplishment one could achieve was the creation of an original Torah thought. Now I know that the greatest accomplishment by far is to make a widow happy" (Rav Chaim Ozer).

Rav Elya Lopian on helping others.

Reb Elyah Lopian instructed his students to fill up the cup for the next boy after washing their hands. In addition to it being a chessed, *it trained the students to be on the lookout for opportunities to help others.*

FRIENDS

FRIENDS-DEFINED

Everyone wants to have lots of friends and be liked and accepted. But regardless of who you are you have probably found that not always does everyone like you and approve of what you are doing. This is normal. And this knowledge is very empowering.

Friends should warm you and enhance your life. Although it is true that friends should challenge each other, the enjoyable times should be most important. Accepting your friends' constructive criticisms will allow them to bring out the best in you. If they excel in one area or another then model yourself after their special attributes. Learn from Sarah's shemiras ha'lashon, Rivkah's neatness, Rochel's helpfulness and so on. Each in her own way can help you become a better person.

CHOOSE YOUR FRIENDS CAREFULLY

Be extremely careful about the friends you associate with. The people you are close to will have a strong influence on your attitudes. People tend to forget their purpose in life when they are in the wrong company (*Mesilas Yesharim*). Take time now to think about your present friends and to consider if you are joyous and involved in Torah oriented thoughts and activities when with them. If a girl is not a positive influence then she is probably not really a good friend. Some friends might be fun to be with, but if they say things that make you uncomfortable, you'll be better off in the long run if you avoid them, or at least cut down on the time you spend with them.

Any relationship in which those involved are not sensitive to each other's needs is merely a superficial relationship. Friendship, by definition, must be based on an awareness of each other's needs and sensitivities.

 Food For Thought

Harav Moshe Leib Sossover, zt"l, was wont to say that he learned the definition of true friendship from a simple, drunken farmer. He heard this man ask his friend, "Do you love me?"

The friend responded, "Of course I do," and he immediately proceeded to demonstrate his affection by embracing and kissing him.

The drunken farmer continued, "Do you know what I am lacking? Do you know what I need?"

"How should I know what you need?"

The friend replied. "Well, if you are not aware of my needs, how can you say that you are my friend?" This story sums it up. A friend is aware; a friend cares. One who is not aware of his friend's needs is not much of a friend.

SEEK OUT HAPPY, SUPPORTIVE FRIENDS

Seek out happy, supportive people with upbeat outlooks and spiritual goals; their positive energy will rub off on you. Such pleasant and considerate people are like tranquilizers for the soul. Not only can you enjoy their company, but you can also learn a lot from them. Observe how effectively they deal with other people and with life's challenges. The attitudes and methods you can pick up and copy just by watching the actions and words of a person with healthy self-esteem can transform your life (Rambam; Gra).

Friendship doubles joy and cuts grief in half. When you share your anxieties with good friends, they will give you support, a fresh perspective and positive suggestions.

Once when Reb Aharon Ha'gadol of Karlin was sitting at his tisch, he sent one of the Chassidim outside to see what was going on in the street and report back. The Chassid reported that he had seen two drunks swaying back and forth, to and fro across the pavement. They were so drunk they could not walk in a straight line. One drunk said to the other: "Here, let's hold each other and this way we won't fall down!" The holy Tzaddik, the Karliner Rebbe immediately taught his Chassidim a lesson from that remark. "Do you hear?! Did you hear what he said? If we each hold onto each other, then we will not fall!"

BEWARE OF POPULARITY

Popularity can be a slippery path. It tends to be fleeting and is usually superficial. This may come as a surprise to you, but trying to be everyone's friend can actually require a huge investment of time and effort. That concentration may force you to do things that make you uncomfortable or that cause friction at home. Although it is important to get along with everyone, you'll accomplish more if you use your time to develop the qualities that will build good solid friendships.

FRIENDS SHOULD HELP YOU STAND TALL

If you are trying to be friends with someone who doesn't feel the same way about you, it may be best to move on. Remember none of us is ever going to get everyone to like us. Try to associate with friends who genuinely like you for what you are. Are the girls you spend time with ridiculing your opinions and destroying your confidence? If so, they are not friends. Friends should help you stand tall.

LEARN TO BE LIKEABLE

If you are having difficulties in getting along with others, pay attention to what you say and do. You may be complaining a lot, or saying sarcastic remarks that you think are cute and funny, but actually others do not appreciate them. Watch how girls with lots of friends interact. Although you do not want to be a copycat, you can learn how to express yourself in a likeable manner. If you need help, speak to your mother, a teacher or someone you admire. Take action – and you can improve!

INVEST IN YOUR FRIENDS

A good friendship is worth investing in. It often means reaching out to others; it also means asking for forgiveness when you have hurt them. Let you friends know how much you like and care about them by complimenting them and helping them out.

> "IF YOU WANT TO UNDERSTAND WHAT A PERSON IS LIKE, ASK WHO HIS FRIENDS ARE"
>
> (RAV MENACHEM MEIRI).

> "FRIENDSHIP IS PAYING CAREFUL ATTENTION TO MY FRIEND, MAKING HIM COMFORTABLE WHEN HE WANTS TO SIT DOWN, AND LISTENING CAREFULLY WHEN HE SPEAKS"
>
> (RAV SHLOMO IBN GAVIROL).

Gilad stood at the door of my resource room looking shy and thoughtful. I ushered him in and sat the ten-year-old opposite me.

"So why are you here?" I asked after I was sure that he was comfortable.

"Because I need help with my school work," he replied.

"Shall we start with your homework?"

We proceeded from one assignment to the next. Clearly this boy knew his stuff. We moved from writing to oral comprehension and he scored well in all areas.

I couldn't figure out what he was doing in my resource

room. When his homework was completed I asked him if there was anything else he wanted to review.

He shook his head. "I think that's all there is for today."

"Okay then. See you around."

"I'll be back for another session tomorrow."

Our second session was a repeat of the first. Clearly this child did not need any help. I decided to speak to his teacher. "I was wondering why Gilad is being sent to see me," I asked him.

"I'm not sending him."

"Then why is he coming to the resource room?"

"Because he wants to come. He tells me that he feels that you are helping him."

I shook my head from side to side. "But he doesn't need my help."

"But if the child feels that he is benefiting from the personal attention, why should it bother you?"

When he put it like that what could I say?

The weeks passed. Finally, one day I decided to confront Gilad. At the end of our session I looked him in the eye and said, "I would like to ask you something."

He waited quietly.

"You know that there is no reason for you to be here, right?"

He didn't reply.

"You don't really need to see me, while you are taking the time of others who do require my help."

Gilad sighed.

"So you are going to tell me?" I prodded.

He lowered his eyes. "Yes."

"Well, I have this friend and he has a hard time in class. It's hard for him to concentrate, and half the time he can't remember what he learned. His parents told him that he was going to have to start coming to the resource room to study with you."

"Hmm," I commented anticipating what was coming next.

"But my friend didn't want to do that. He told me that only nerds go to resource rooms and that they're for stupid people. He absolutely refused to cooperate." He paused. "But I knew that he needs to come here. So I told him that going to a resource room is not a big deal and that I go there too. Once I told him that, I had to keep my word and actually go."

He looked me in the eye.

I felt a tear in the corner of my eye. "I am really glad that we had the opportunity to get to know one another."

Gilad smiled (Class Acts 2 pages 273-277).

Many of you have seen that smile when he and his two friends were kidnapped and eventually murdered al Kiddush Hashem.

A story of true friendship.

It was the day before camp and Miriam Esther was busy with last minute preparations. One minute she was packing and the next someone accidentally slammed into Miriam Esther, hitting her nose. She collapsed in an agony of pain. In a short time, her nose was terribly swollen. Her pediatrician took one look at the puffy mass and declared that there was nothing he could do. "No one will be able to examine your nose for at least 72 hours," he explained.

When he heard that she was headed to camp he advised her to send him a picture of her nose after the *swelling went down. Her pediatrician ended up advising her to see a specialist. Her parents found someone who was able to adjust her nose back into place. He then placed a large, cumbersome cast on top.*

Miriam Esther was mortified when she glanced at her ridiculous reflection in the mirror. She was overcome by the pain and anticipated humiliation.

How could she return to her job as a waitress wearing this ridiculous-looking cast on her face? Every girl would be staring at her. The questions and comments would be too much to bear.

Emotionally and physically drained Miriam Esther returned to camp late Tuesday night. In the morning, she swallowed her pride and headed to the dining room to do her job. It wasn't easy for her to enter the camp dining room.

What she encountered was a scene she will never forget. Every single waitress was wearing a faux bandage on her face.

They had decided that they weren't going to let their friend deal with the shame and awkwardness. They were in this together.

The gesture brought tears to Miriam Esther's eyes. The sensitivity and understanding of her friends meant the world to her (R' Yitzchok Hisiger, Yated 15 of Av 5776).

STANDING UP FOR WHAT IS RIGHT

WHERE DID OUR COURAGE GO?

We are all born with the sense of confidence in ourselves. Why then is there so little courage and self-expression around us? How did we lose our confidence and our personality? When did we start to believe that others know better than we do? When did we start to copy other people's behavior? When did we start to dress approximately the same, just because a designer decided that purple or green is the color of the year?

How did we come to a place where we trust others more than ourselves? It starts with not standing up for what we believe in. Being a servant of Hashem requires that you not cave into pressures that would lead you away from what is important.

DON'T LOSE RESPECT FOR YOURSELF

Being silent makes you weak and cowardly. You will think twice before standing up next time, and this will eventually become one of your regrets in life. If you bow to others and their opinions, and do things their way, whether right or not, you start to lose your own identity and forget your goals. The less you allow yourself to think freely and develop your own understanding of what Hashem expects of you, the more you become a follower, losing your own direction along the way. Your own thoughts become uncertain and hard to hear. If you give into others and compromise on your values, you are going to lose respect for yourself.

TAKE FULL RESPONSIBILITY

It takes courage to stand up for what is right in a "copy-paste" society. Sometimes you need to stand up to your friends. It would be easier to bury your head in the sand and hope things pass you over without the need to make your opinion heard; but if you really know that something is the right thing to do, when you are sure that *halachah* and *mesorah* are on your side, then you must stand up for what you believe.

The more you stand up for your beliefs, the more self-respect you will develop and the less you will rely on others to validate your decisions. You'll reinforce your independence and ability to stand on your own two feet without anyone else to support you.

You have a brain and a mind of your own, use it. If you don't take full responsibility for the totality of your actions, then how can you expect others to? The person who you should always be able to count on to stand up for you – no matter what – is you. Your standing up for what is right not only makes you feel good, it inspires others. Your determination ignites the determination of others. You will never know the extents of the ripple effects you generate.

"IF I AM I BECAUSE I AM I (WITHOUT WORRYING ABOUT WHAT YOU WILL THINK OF ME), AND YOU ARE YOU BECAUSE YOU ARE YOU (WITHOUT WORRYING WHAT I WILL THINK OF YOU) – THEN I AM TRULY I AND YOU ARE TRULY YOU. IF, ON THE OTHER HAND, I AM I BECAUSE YOU ARE YOU (I AM TRYING TO BE THE PERSON WHO WILL PLEASE YOU) AND YOU ARE YOU BECAUSE I AM I (YOU ARE TRYING TO BE THE PERSON WHO WILL PLEASE ME), THEN I AM NOT I AND YOU ARE NOT YOU" (THE KOTZKER REBBE).

Ask Yourself:

Am I doing this because it is a trend or because it is the right thing to do?

Am I doing it because it is what I want to do or what they want me to do?

Will I regret it tomorrow, if I don't do something about it today?

Remember that it is the choices we make today that make us the people we eventually become.

 Food For Thought

Hashem doesn't ask us to become angels. He has enough angels. "*Ve'anshei kodesh tihiyu li*" He wants us to become "holy individuals"; individuals who fight for their spiritual growth and ultimate holiness (Kotzker Rebbe).

The *Chazon Ish* gives *chizuk* to his sister.

The Steipler Gaon insisted that his daughters wear long dresses that covered well past their knees. He wanted to ensure that his children would be completely be'tznius at all times. In those days, most of the girls and women in their community wore shorter skirts and dresses.

Once the Steipler Rebbetzin told her brother, the Chazon Ish, "It disturbs me that my daughters look different than the other children in the neighborhood. I would like them to look more like the rest of the girls."

The Chazon Ish smiled and told the Rebbetzin, "Do you think it is your daughters that are dressed differently? They are the ones dressing properly and doing what is right. It is the other girls, the ones not dressed properly, who are different! You should not worry about what others say about you. It is they who must worry about being different!" (Oz Ve'hadar)

Doing the right thing:

Yanky and Shmueli took their responsibility as head counselors of a summer program for American bochurim visiting Eretz Yisroel very seriously. They squeezed as much fun as they could into the structured program of shiurim and lectures. This sometimes involved staying up late and getting up very early.

At six a.m., the morning of a scheduled trip kayaking down the Jordan River, Yanky made a calculated decision to turn his alarm off. The campers had not gotten to bed until three a.m.; there was no way he was waking them this early – trip or no trip.

At 8:30 Shmueli opened one eye and glanced at the time. While washing his hands he called out to Yanky. "Do you think we can still go?"

"I'm not sure," Yanky replied.

"Let's try."

The boys were quickly woken. They hurriedly dressed. They davened and ate on the bus. The roads were still basically traffic free.

When they arrived Yanky and Shmueli hurried over to the cashiers to assess the situation.

"Lots of people out already?"

"No. You're the first group today."

"So the water's empty right now?"

The cashier nodded.

They paid and everyone headed down the slope to the departure point where they received their life jackets and oars.

The boys had a blast both in and out of the boats. Their laughter and song bounced off the sharp-edged bushes that lined the shore. All too soon they reached the end of the route. Everyone pulled over to the side, disembarked and made their way over to the pickup point to await the shuttle bus that would transport them back to the parking lot and the waiting bus.

The shuttle bus arrived and when all were seated, the driver turned the ignition key. Before he could take off however, three additional people appeared on the horizon. They were not boys and their mode of dress left much to be desired. Yanky realized that there was no way he could allow his campers to share a ride with them.

He went over to the driver. "Could you please do me a favor?"

"What did you have in mind?"

"Could we please leave right now?"

The driver immediately realized what the problem was. "What, and leave those three customers waiting while I return your group to the parking lot?"

"Exactly."

He shook his head. "Sorry. It's against the rules. This bus is for all patrons of the boat rentals. There's no way I can turn someone away, just because you have a problem with the way they're dressed."

"Look, sir," Yanky protested, "these boys are religious. They are yeshivah students. It would not be fair to subject them to sights which they try so hard to avoid."

At this point the three newcomers had already arrived at the bus. A voice inside Yanky's head told him to stop arguing.

"Don't make such a big deal about this," it said. "They're going to hear you. It's a chillul Hashem."

Another voice answered the first voice. "It's not a chillul Hashem. I am in charge of these bachurim. There is no way I can do this to them. It would be wrong. That would be a chillul Hashem!"

Yanky closed his eyes. "What would the Ribono Shel Olam want me to do?" he asked himself. Then he knew. "I'm sorry sir. Please allow us to get off the bus. This is nothing personal. I am sure everyone on this bus is a nice, wonderful person but I cannot allow my boys to travel under these circumstances."

"It's a long walk back to the parking lot," the driver warned.

"Thanks for your concern," Yanky replied. Then they all got off and stood watching as the bus pulled away through a cloud of exhaust.

With Yanky leading the way they began walking down the road towards the parking lot.

Everyone walked in silence. The episode had put a damper on everyone's mood.

Suddenly, they saw a cloud of dust approaching. It was the bus that had left them at the stop. It came to a sudden screeching halt right beside them. The door swung open. It was the same driver.

"Hop aboard!" the driver greeted the boys.

"What about the three passengers?"

"I asked one of my friends to take them back to the parking lot."

"Why did you change your mind?"

"I thought about what you said, and I realized that you had a point. If you want to shield your eyes from sights of impurity, I should be congratulating you, not making things harder for you. You are trying to act the *way a Jew should act. I felt that I should support that, so I returned."*

The boys laughed as they jostled one another to get on board. Hashem had sent a messenger to let them know that what was right was right (Class Acts 2 pages 266-271).

DON'T PUT YOURSELF AT THE MERCY OF OTHERS

DON'T TIE YOUR HAPPINESS TO OTHERS

You'll never get anywhere if you sit around waiting for someone else to tell you you're okay. If you want to live a happy life, don't tie your happiness to people. You wouldn't worry so much about what others think of you if you realize how seldom they really give you any thought. When you are content with yourself you don't need other people's approval.

CONFIDENCE NEEDS TO COME FROM WITHIN

Don't construct your life around your friends. The day

will come when your friends will not be the main focus of your life. Confidence needs to come from within not from others. Similarly, don't allow others to dampen your mood. Repeat to yourself, "I will not let _____ decide how I am going to feel." Don't let other people's realities take up too much space in your mind.

DON'T LOOK OVER YOUR SHOULDERS

Life is not a competition. Craving the possessions and abilities of others only leads to unhappiness. Those who spend their time looking over their shoulders to see what their friends have will always feel that they are missing something. To be happy within ourselves should actually be natural and easy. The trouble is that we want to be happier than the other person. That is much more difficult, for we always think the other person is happier than he really is.

It helps if we remember that Hashem would never favor one child over another. You will always find someone who has more than you in specific areas, but you are not seeing the whole picture. We can't in this world. There is so much we don't know. We must feel safe and cared for in the knowledge that Hashem is giving us exactly what we need to serve Him. He is doing that for everyone else as well.

YOU CAN'T PLEASE EVERYONE

It is so easy to be caught up in a whole bunch of worries. When you worry about being accepted by others, you are judging yourself by the opinions of individuals whose moods, attitudes and values are constantly changing. Consider how ridiculous it is to place your happiness in the hands of people who are themselves worried about how others will relate to them. You will constantly be investing huge amounts of energy into pleasing first one person, then another. You are trying to be one person in the morning, another during the day, and yet a third in the evening. Sometimes you will feel pressured into doing things that are opposed to your inner will. This will leave you feeling empty and degraded.

Food For Thought

A person who truly has "everything" is one who is satisfied with his minimum requirement of food and clothing and perceives the Creator as the center of his world (Rav Shlomo Wolbe).

If you are feeling small compared to others then look inside to heal what is going on there.

Think about the well-known story of the stonecutter who was not happy with his lot. After becoming a king, the sun, a cloud and then a mountain, he just wanted to be a stonecutter again! Through all of these roles, he realized the foolishness of his dissatisfaction (Sichos Kodesh Spinka).

YOU ARE SMART

YOU ARE SMARTER THAN YOU THINK

When I am having a bad day everyone looks smarter than me. Always remember that you are smarter than you think and know more than you believe you do. Just because a person doesn't do very well at school doesn't mean that he isn't intelligent. It takes a lot more than high marks to prove the intelligence of a person. Text book learning does not reflect a person's total knowledge. Some hear and remember, some read and remember and others experience and learn.

EVERYBODY IS SMART IN DIFFERENT WAYS

A smart person is not necessarily one who has mastered a lot of material but is one who has developed her talents and aptitudes. Plenty of people who are unsuccessful students do extremely well at life using the other kinds of knowledge they possess. Everybody is smart in different ways. In the real world, there are many lessons which can be learned many ways. You may have a lot of street smarts and people skills which count for more in the long run. You may be talented in many other ways.

APPLY WHAT YOU HAVE LEARNED

Wisdom is an ongoing process. It is the product of the lifelong attempt to acquire wisdom. It is not only the accumulation of knowledge but perhaps even more importantly in the ability to take what you know and effectively and persistently apply it. In other words being smart is the measure of what you do with what you know. Some people are very smart, but do not know how to apply what they know. If you are able to motivate people, get along with them and cheer them, such skills can be more valuable than being 'smart'.

 Avoid phrases like "I wish I were able to..." "If only I were..." "I would try, but..."

Remind yourself repeatedly that you are a competent, bright person with many talents. Expect the best from yourself. The seeds of achievement await your cultivation. If fostered, they will carry you to the heights. Create thought habits that will help you become who you want to be. Use your talents to have a successful life.

Reuven buys a vessel from a non-Jew and sells it to Shimon, believing it to be an inexpensive metal container. Shimon later discovers that it is pure silver. Does

Shimon have to pay Reuven more money?

Shimon owes Reuven nothing. Since Reuven was unaware that he had a silver vessel, he never really owned a silver vessel. The same applies to a person who is unaware of his true value; he therefore has no greatness (Hagahos Ashri)**.**

In his book *Enthusiasm*, Rabbi Z. Pliskin tells the story of a yeshivah boy whose insightful teacher transformed his life.

He once received a mark of fifty on a Gemara exam. The teacher pointed out that the fifty percent of the test he had answered had been answered well.

"Keep up the good work," the teacher said, focusing on what he had answered correctly.

The boy was really surprised at the teacher's comment. The next week he once again got a fifty. He was certain the teacher would reprimand him for not doing better. Instead, he said with a smile, "You answered half the questions. Look at how well you answered question number nineteen. It was a difficult question and your response shows the high intelligence you have been gifted with. Keep up the good work." He had to admit that the teacher was right. He had answered a very difficult question and he had answered it well.

That week he was motivated to utilize more of his G-d given intelligence. He paid attention and reviewed diligently. He mastered the material and he got a perfect mark of 100 on the next test. This time he didn't need the teacher's encouragement. He felt encouraged because of the results he had achieved.

He kept getting high marks. As he matured, he came to realize that it was his teacher's words of encouragement that had made all the difference.

SELF-MASTERY

STANDING UP TO THE YETZER HARA

We are taught that a person who overcomes his desires is stronger than one who overcomes his enemies. Most people who have made significant contributions credit their ability to do so to their disciplined upbringing. Self-mastery requires that you gather your resources, rally your faculties, marshal your energies and focus on doing the will of Hashem.

To make the right choices you must work at controlling your negative tendencies. In everyday activities, it translates into resisting temptation, opposing cravings and thus acquiring good character. It includes things like getting up as soon as your alarm rings, controlling your temper or disciplining yourself to do your homework. It is a process that continues throughout life as you clarify and deepen your understanding of how to stand up to the *yetzer hara*.

 Food For Thought

A person who has not labored to identify and correct his negative character traits is like a blind person who has never seen light (Rav Yisroel Salanter).

REVEAL THE POSITIVE WITHIN

Within each negative character trait lies a positive inner core. The negativity is like a peel, which needs only to be removed to disclose the shinning kernel (Rav Yaakov Meir Schechter). Rabi Akiva's personal growth demonstrates the principal. He was a radical hater of Torah and its scholars for many years and then became a passionate lover of Torah. The love was hidden within his heart waiting to be revealed (*Ki Atah Imadi*, Vol. 3 page 172).

The Piasetzna Rebbe, Rabbi Kalonymos Kalman Shapiro, compares character improvement to fighting a carefully planned war, where strategy is developed based on honest and thorough research. See what is really holding back improvement, and then find a way to overcome the barrier. If one tactic does not work, try another and yet another. It must always remain on the front burner, for if you do not conquer yourself, you will be conquered by yourself. When your desires are in control of you, they color your words, actions and thoughts in a negative way. The undisciplined person is a slave to his or her own weaknesses.

Even worse, others will easily conquer you. It is up to you to choose your master. Choose yourself!

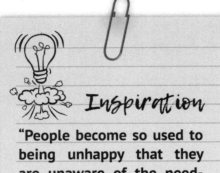

Inspiration

"People become so used to being unhappy that they are unaware of the needless misery they cause themselves. They imprison themselves by filling their minds with thoughts of resentment, hatred, and envy. It is amazing how they tolerate living such a life. The only reason they do tolerate it is because they have become so used to living with these thoughts that they feel it's normal. They think it's impossible for life to be any different!" (Rav Yerucham Levovitz).

"MUSAR SHREIT, GEVALD, BEIT ZICH! THE STUDY OF MUSSAR SHOUTS, "CHANGE!'"

(RAV CHAIM SHMULEVITZ)

SATISFYING RESULTS

You earn your value by practicing self-mastery. When you are your master, no one will have the power to enslave you. You are freed from laziness, weakness, fear and doubt.

It is the only way to acquire true wisdom. It allows you to develop your individuality and your talents. The results are so satisfying. The payoff is steady growth, as you move closer and closer to Hashem.

A businessman hired a driver to take him to the fair. It was a warm summer day, and the swaying carriage soon rocked the businessman to sleep. Before long, the driver found his head nodding, and he too was sound asleep.

As soon as the horses realized that the reins were lax, they began drifting to the side of the road, stopping to nibble on plants that caught their attention. Then the horses spotted a lush patch of grass and galloped toward it, overturning the wagon in the process.

The driver and passenger found themselves rudely awakened.

"What happened?" the driver called out.

"What happened?" the businessman angrily snapped back. "The wagon turned over! Can't you see?"

"I will whip the horses," the driver said trying to scramble to his feet.

"It is you who deserves a beating," the passenger declared. "You are the one at fault for letting go of the reins!"

"Me?" the driver protested. "I saw that the horses were proceeding down the road, and I assumed that they would continue as they should.

"Who would have imagined that they would abandon the path?"

The businessman was enraged. "You aren't making any sense! Horses are only animals. How can you rely *on them to know the way? As long as they feel that a firm hand holds the reins, they stay on course. But when the grip loosens, they do as they please."*

The body is like that animal. If the soul is in control, then all is well, but if the soul loosens its grip then the body will throw its master into a ditch (Rav Moshe of Coucy).

GROWTH IS ENERGIZING

The process of changing levels and moving on to the next level, which we refer to as growth, is demanding. The refinement of character, which results from this growth process, gives rise to true joy. In every situation try to visualize what type of growth Hashem is seeking from you. The realization that Hashem has assigned a particular challenge to you out of His desire for your spiritual growth is very energizing and creates within you an additional attachment to Him.

"IF A PERSON INSISTS ON HAVING EVERYTHING HE WISHES, THE LACK OF EVEN A SMALL PLEASURE CAN MAKE HIM FEEL EXTREMELY UNHAPPY" (MICHTAV ME'ELIYAHU).

STRETCH YOURSELF

There are no shortcuts. Ease and comfort may be painless, but that is not the goal of living! Life's deepest and most enduring delights are achieved by stretching yourself to grow, moving beyond your comfort zone to bring out your potential. Effort makes the desired result truly gratifying.

If you limit the bother of striving, you rob yourself of the authentic fulfillment that comes through hard work and achievement.

Never give up on aspirations for greatness because of the amount of time it will take to reach your goal, because time has a way of passing no matter what you do.

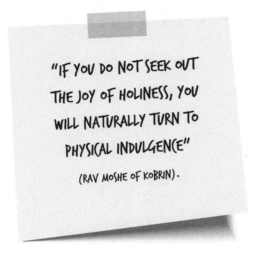

"IF YOU DO NOT SEEK OUT THE JOY OF HOLINESS, YOU WILL NATURALLY TURN TO PHYSICAL INDULGENCE"

(RAV MOSHE OF KOBRIN).

The more you involve yourself in the spiritual, and the higher your spiritual level, the less need you have for the material. The more importance a person attaches to the material world, the less interest and appreciation he will have for the spiritual.

PATIENCE

PRACTICE MAKES PERFECT

Anyone can get angry but only notable people remain calm in difficult situations. It is well worth practicing ignoring trivial irritations. For example, try being more patient with a sibling who walks into your room without knocking. Maybe your mother makes you do something around the house that you don't like to do but it must be done. Maybe the sister who shares your room has legitimate demands that you find objectionable. As often as you can, cooperate without feeling or acting annoyed. This way you will get practice dealing with the more irritating day-to-day annoyances.

TAKE TIME TO THINK

Although your immediate emotional response might be anger, imagine a huge stop sign or press an imaginary pause button. It should take about 90 seconds for the angry response to clear.

You will have time to think. Remind yourself that these 'undesirable' challenges were placed in our life only for the good. Ultimately, there is no place for anger, no place for worry, and no place for fear. We no longer have to deal with regrets and "If only's" when we are conscious of the fact that all is from Hashem. We become more serene and accepting of "bad" events, realizing that it is all a part of a perfect Divine plan. When you expend less negative energy on those events, your life will be so much more enjoyable.

OPPORTUNITIES TO BECOME GREAT

Don't say to yourself, "Not again, I can't stand this!" Instead say, "here's another chance to build my strength; here's another opportunity to become great." You need to ask yourself, "Am I putting my *emunah* into practice in all phases of my daily routine?" As you look for things that have been misplaced, react to a hurtful statement, experience a loss of money, deal with

Inspiration

My dear Friend!
It is not my custom to involve myself in arguments or contention. Differences in thought lead to differences in action, so why complain about the deeds of others when we know that their opinions were established decades ago? The consequences of a lifetime of influence cannot simply be erased (Letters of the Chazon Ish).

someone who has disturbed your sleep, or wait in a long line, you must train yourself to lift your eyes and heart to Heaven and acknowledge that all that happens is orchestrated by Hashem for your benefit. Always remember that a person does not stub his toe below unless it is decreed Above - even if the toe stubbing is caused by means of a human being with free will (*Chullin* 7b; Chozeh of Lublin).

> The *Sefas Emes* was seeing off a chassid at the train station. The chassid asked for some words as a parting memento.
>
> The Rebbe replied, "Do you know how that steam locomotive has enough power to pull all those carriages? Because it keeps the steam inside" (Sipurei Chassidim).

ANOTHER CHANCE TO PROVE YOURSELF

Because we are here to prove ourselves, we cannot expect life to go as smoothly as we would like. Friends will say the wrong things, your teacher will reprimand you, and your sister will spoil your surprise. But remember! Every situation has been tailor made for you to help you grow and develop your character. It is up to you to choose not to get upset over it, but rather view it as another chance to prove yourself. As we develop spiritually, internalizing the truth that everything is from Hashem and all for our benefit, our emotions become more settled. Eternal reward awaits the person who does not get frustrated when he encounters these endless daily challenges. Blowing these things out of proportion will harm your sanity, your friendships and your happiness.

Rav Yitzchok Zilberstein records a story told by a young man from Bnei Brak:

My wife and I and our five children were planning to eat the first Rosh Hashanah meal at the home of my in-laws at the other end of Bnei Brak. Our plan was to be ready early and call a taxi.

Unfortunately, my wife's Yom Tov preparations took much longer than expected. Just when we thought that we could finally call a taxi, one child needed a diaper change, another was very hungry and a third threw a tantrum.

By the time they were settled, it was too late to call a taxi. We would have to walk, which meant that we would arrive at our destination after dark and I would be late for Ma'ariv.

As we left the house, the atmosphere was tense. I couldn't help but be upset. Angry thoughts swirled inside of my head, "Is this how one begins the New Year - by walking into shul in the middle of Ma'ariv? Why couldn't my wife have begun her preparations earlier?"

Baruch Hashem. I managed to think the matter through clearly. I knew that anything that I would say now would be like a knife in my wife's heart. As the New Year was being ushered in, I was standing on a spiritual precipice.

I decided that I would focus on all the good that my wife does for me, and in this way, my frustration would dissipate. I had a whole year's time to ensure that the situation would not repeat itself next Rosh Hashanah. In the meantime, the only expectation that Hashem had of me was that I should remain silent about what had happened.

At that holy time, when every Jew seeks to find favor in Hashem's eyes through teshuvah, my teshuvah would be to control myself and not to express my anger by saying something hurtful.

When I finally arrived at my father-in-law's shul, the minyan was already past Shema. I felt bad about this, but I sincerely believe that I had faithfully fulfilled my true obligation.

During the following year, I saw tremendous success wherever I turned. Everything I touched seemed to turn to gold. I am certain that this was related to my big test on Rosh Hashanah.

LIVE IN THE PRESENT

EACH MORNING IS A NEW BEGINNING

Each morning should be the messenger of a new beginning. View each day as a page in your autobiography, and start a fresh page each morning with the assurance that the unfolding day will bring great things. Anticipation of pleasure can only increase your joy.

When you anticipate that something will be pleasant, you are more likely to enjoy it and that pleasure will be more exciting and more real.

"Today is going to be a great day!" Use this anticipation to energize yourself.

Who will you meet today, what will you encounter, and

what will you achieve?

THE MOMENTS OF YOUR LIFE ARE PRECIOUS

The past is now memories. The future is hopeful illusions. We must focus on the present. This is the only true reality. Focus on the present and determine what you can do for Hashem. The moments of your life are your most treasured possessions. Don't agonize over yesterday and don't worry about tomorrow. Make the best of the present as you seize its blessing. The current moment is precious, never to return. Try to give your very best to the world every day. Don't settle for any substitutes. Contentment slips through the fingers of those who waste their time dreaming about another time, a different place, or better circumstances.

> Someone once commented to the Chazon Ish that the entire world is like a dream.
> The Chazon Ish replied, "It is like a dream for those who are sleeping." However, for those who understand the value of life the world is very real and absolutely wonderful (Rav Elimelech Biderman).

TODAY IS NEVER RETRIEVABLE

One of the biggest mistakes people make is assuming that tomorrow is going to be more important than today. What a silly notion! Today is real. You are here today and there is so much you can do. If you miss the spiritual progress you can experience today, it is never retrievable. There are no such guarantees with regard to tomorrow. Concentrate on the present moment; take joy in it and give it all you've got.

Say to yourself, "I am exactly where I need to be right now!" When your spirits are up you look at the world in a brighter and more focused way.

HASHEM SMOOTHS OUT THE BUMPS

You must constantly thank Hashem for what He has done for you in the past and make your requests for what you want in the future (*Berachos 54a*). By regularly speaking to Hashem you reinforce the understanding that Hashem is there behind the scenes, smoothing out the bumps and guiding you through what you experience as your failures.

"IF A PERSON DESIRES CONTENTMENT, HE SHOULD STRIVE TO EMBRACE EVERYTHING THAT HAPPENS TO HIM. ALL SHOULD BE EQUAL IN HIS EYES. THIS WILL LEAD TO ONGOING HAPPINESS"

(REBBE REB BUNIM OF P'SHISCHA).

SLOW DOWN

Living in the present can also mean slowing down sometimes. Instead of being busy running around to sales and rushing from one conversation to another, spend some time with your family. Visit your grandmother. Spend some quiet time with yourself. Remember that Hashem is to be found in silence.

Ask Yourself:

Do I have regular activities that you find meaningful?

What changes can I introduce to my current schedule which will make my life more pleasurable?

THE VALUE OF TIME

The Imrei Emes looked on his watch as a most trusted companion. He once gave his watch to the watchmaker to be repaired only because it fell behind a few seconds each day. When a young newlywed came to the Rebbe to ask which mussar text he should study, the Imrei Emes pointed to his watch and said, "this is the biggest mussar text - every minute that passes never comes back."

The Imrei Emes often remarked, "Why do we give a bridegroom a gold watch as a gift? To teach him that each minute and second is worth more than gold."

A young man once asked Rav Chaim Kanievsky how he manages to receive so many people in an hour.

Rav Chaim replied, "There are 60 minutes in an hour and 60 seconds in a minute. That is 3,600 seconds. Do you know how much can be done in 3,600 seconds?"
(Tuvcha Yabiu)

DON'T WORRY ABOUT THE FUTURE

HASHEM WRITES THE SCRIPTS

Some people are experts at using their imagination to create all types of worrisome scenarios. When you recognize that you do not write the scripts of your life, nor do you direct all the action, it becomes apparent that there is really nothing to worry about. But why can't you get rid of the fear?

HASHEM WILL SOLVE OUR PROBLEMS

Emunah is the antidote to fear. Remember that Hashem

is more powerful than any entity. He can offer solutions to problems that appear impossible. Hashem is close by to save us in times of trouble (*Peleh Yoetz*). Leave the solutions to our problems in Hashem's hands. Hashem has been kind and compassionate to you even when you may not have deserved it, and He will certainly continue to help you now. In a calm state, it is possible to serenely look for positive developments. A person's suffering is precisely measured; it's given orders when to arrive and when to leave (*Avodah Zarah* 55).

My husband and I take turns reminding each other that when a person sighs as if to say, "What will be," that is *apikorsus*. Keep repeating to yourself, "Hashem is running the world, and that's the way He wants things. Everything is for the best." It is then possible to lift one's eyes to Hashem, confident that things will improve and that his fortunes will visibly change for the better.

> "ONE WHO WORRIES ABOUT THE FUTURE WILL NEVER FIND SATISFACTION. WHEN THE FUTURE BECOMES THE PRESENT, HE WILL WORRY ABOUT A LATER FUTURE" (MADREIGAS HA'ADAM).

WITH EMUNAH THERE IS NO DESPAIR

Small problems, as well as seemingly overwhelming

problems, are all the same to Hashem. A person who is firm in his faith finds it possible to transfer all his burdens from his own shoulders, so that he no longer feels such a tremendously weighty responsibility for everything that happens to him. After that, no situation leads to despair.

WORRY IS RIDICULOUS

Imagine meeting someone who looks very unhappy. When you ask, he tells you that everything is fine in his life right now, but that he is worrying about something that might happen in another ten years. Wouldn't you question his sanity? Surely, everyone would agree that it is ridiculous to worry about something so far in the future! But you do not seem to realize that worrying now about next week is precisely the same thing.

> THE LASHON HAKODESH WORD FOR WORRY –DAAGAH– IS MADE UP OF THE FIRST FIVE LETTERS OF THE ALPHABET, EXCLUDING THE LETTER BEIS. BEIS STANDS FOR BITACHON (TRUST). A PERSON WITH DAAGAH IS LACKING BITACHON IN HASHEM.

WORRY IS A WASTE OF TIME

Worry is contagious. It has a detrimental effect on you

and on everyone in your environment. If something can be done to rectify the situation, then take action. Unfortunately, people often worry about things they cannot change. Many times, a person would hardly suffer from a given situation if he hadn't worried in the first place! Remind yourself of how many times disaster loomed in the past and Hashem intervened to improve matters dramatically.

SCHEDULE WORRY PERIODS

When you have a problem, you will find that even fifteen minutes of scheduled thinking time is more productive than hours and hours of distracted worrying while you work on something else. Consider jotting a brief note to yourself so you will remember to think about a problem. Then set aside a certain time for problem solving. When your mind takes you to that worrying place, remind yourself that you will deal with it in the designated time. Set your difficulties aside and continue with your life.

In your designated worrying time form a mental image of your best option and determine how you can accomplish it. Consider the worst-case scenario. In most cases, you will realize that it is not as bad as you initially thought. After that, move your thoughts back to the present.

> "THE PAST CAN'T BE CHANGED. MANY OF THE SCENARIOS YOU WORRY ABOUT NEVER OCCUR OR END UP FAR BETTER THAN YOU EXPECTED" (RAMBAM).

A poor peddler trudged along the road, bowed down by the heavy weight of the sack he carried on his back. A rich merchant, passing by in his comfortable carriage, took pity on the poor man and offered him a ride.

The peddler clambered into the carriage and sank gratefully onto the bench, thanking the merchant profusely. As the journey resumed, however, the merchant saw that the peddler still clutched his heavy sack.

"Why don't you put down your bundle?" the merchant suggested. "You can keep it on the seat next to you, or on the floor."

"Oh, I couldn't do that," the peddler demurred. "You're already doing so much for me. I couldn't possibly ask you to carry my heavy sack, too!"

The merchant laughed. "Don't be foolish! The carriage is carrying both you and your bundle. You don't need to tire yourself unnecessarily by carrying your burden on your shoulder!" (Dubno Maggid)

Those who live with a firm belief that Hashem is in charge, live a happier life. Like the passengers on a train or bus, they are confident that each turn of the wheel brings them closer to their desired destination. They can lean back comfortably in their seats and enjoy the ride.

BUILDING YOUR RELATIONSHIP WITH HASHEM

IT IS ALWAYS GOOD

One who has *emunah* is truly full of life, and his days are always filled with good. You will benefit tremendously by working on your relationship with Hashem. When things go well, it is certainly good. When one has troubles, it is also good. Rest assured with the knowledge that when Hashem withholds something, were you to have it, it would cause you harm (Rav S.R. Hirsch).

KEEP HASHEM ON YOUR RADAR SCREEN

Make an effort to speak to Him in your own words

asking Him for all your wants and needs. Trusting in Hashem requires that you keep Hashem on your radar screen for things both big and small. Keep your eyes open for the numerous instances of Hashem's Divine Providence throughout each day.

HASHEM IS CHEERING YOU ON

Remember that Hashem hovers over you everywhere. Imagine that He is cheering you on. All you need to do is acknowledge His presence and reach out to Him through the uncertainty. His illuminating hand will be waiting to receive you. Such *bitachon* girds us with phenomenal inner strength and the conviction that there is no situation on earth, no matter how terrible, where Hashem cannot come to our rescue (*Shomrei Emunim*).

Any situation, once properly understood, can be a means of coming nearer to Hashem. In the real world, you are subject to numerous small irritations and criticisms. You are going to lose things and make mistakes and encounter plans gone awry again and again. When you internalize that Hashem is in charge, you free yourself from the distress that comes with these incidents. When you internalize that you are not alone, you never need to worry whether you made the right

> "KEEP CALLING OUT TO YOUR HEAVENLY FATHER. THE MORE YOU CALL TO YOUR FATHER, THE MORE HE WILL ASSUME THAT ROLE"
>
> (MAGGID OF MEZRITSCH).

choice. This faith enables you to avoid the pitfalls of confusion and loss of nerve that comes with lack of trust.

Food For Thought

"Taste and see Hashem's goodness" (*Tehillim* 21:19). The expression "taste and see" comes to teach us that someone who tastes something is able to understand if it is good. So too, someone who trusts in Hashem will recognize the very great goodness of Hashem and merit experiencing Hashem's goodness on a regular basis.

YOU ARE NEVER ALONE

"The greatest reward for faith in Hashem is for Hashem to place strength and courage in one's heart, which will engender a stronger faith. One might think that it would be more

"IF A JEW TRULY UNDERSTOOD WHAT IT MEANT TO HAVE AN ETERNAL EXISTENCE, HE WOULD BE SO HAPPY THAT HE WOULD RUSH INTO THE STREET AND DANCE THE COSSACKS' DANCE LIKE A LUNATIC" (BAAL SHEM TOV).

useful to merit wealth, for then he would never need to worry. But material wealth does not free a person of worry. Even if a person could create gold, he would still live in fear of robbers and murderers. However, a person with faith has peace of mind. Therefore, the greatest reward Hashem could grant the person with faith is strength and courage, as a result of which he will place his hope in Hashem in greater measure" (The Brisker Rav, Rav Yitzchok Zeev Soloveitchik).

> The Klausenberger Rebbe lost everything in the Holocaust, including his wife and eleven children. He conveyed, in one sentence, the secret of how he could overcome his suffering: "I lost all my family - I lost everything - but I haven't lost Hakadosh Baruch Hu."

A marvelous exercise to increase awareness.

> After Rabbi Noach Weinberg's death, a student told of a nightly ritual he had advised her to introduce to her household. Each evening after tucking her child in, she would help the child put together a list of people in the world who loved her - Mommy, Tatty, Zeidy and Bubby as well as all the important people in her life. Each evening the last question was always the same: "Who loves you most of all?" Together they would shout, "Hashem!"

Dovid Hamelech informs us, *Hashem Mi'shamayim hishkif...liros hayaish maskil doresh es Elokim*—"Hashem looked down from Heaven to see if there is a wise man who seeks Hashem" (Tehillim 14:2). Hashem is looking to see who is thinking about him. He sees millions and millions of people and almost nobody is thinking about Him.

There is no need to publicize our thoughts. As it says, "*Vehatznea leches im Elokecha*" (Micha 6:8). If we were to advertise our intentions, we may be doing it because we want people to praise us. When we walk modestly with Hashem, nobody knows what we are thinking about.

YOU AND YOUR BODY

RESIST MEDIA STEREOTYPES

It is a fact that there are as many different types of beauty as there are people in the world. The media would have you believe otherwise. Unfortunately, you live in a world where you are encouraged to feel inadequate. Advertisers bring you to a place where you think your hair is damaged, your skin is flawed, your body disfigured. They insist that you have to be super slim or you shouldn't feel good about yourself. In order to look a certain way you need the right clothes, specific skin products and you must style your hair a certain way.

LIKE YOURSELF THE WAY YOU ARE

As ridiculous as this sounds, most people follow the leader. People actually believe that they can't look good unless they have the right look. There is a lot of pressure to look good, especially for girls, but it is not a good idea to let the drive for beauty have too much power in your life. The way to fight back against this pressure is to like yourself just the way you are. Once you make this decision, you will feel better about yourself because you are the one making the decision.

There is nothing as attractive as a big smile. So stand up straight and tall and appreciate the way you look. Our interior beauty is what makes our exterior beautiful.

EAT RIGHT

Taking proper care of yourself is part of your divine assignment. Your body will serve you well if you take good care of it. Just as overeating foods is not conducive to good health neither is undereating. You feel better physically, emotionally and spiritually when you eat the right things. If you are hungry, you deserve to eat healthy food so you feel good. Food helps fuel all your spiritual activities.

> One evening a joyous farbrengen was held at the home of Rabbi Shmuel Betzalel Sheftel. Rabbi Shmuel Betzalel instructed that the lamb being raised in his yard should be slaughtered and hot stew prepared to fuel the farbrengen.
>
> The next morning Rabbi Shmuel Betzalel's wife asked where the lamb had disappeared to.
>
> Rabbi Shmuel Betzalel replied, "The lamb has not disappeared. It has only changed its sound. Yesterday

it said, 'Baa Baa'; today it is saying 'Echo-odd!' O-one!'"
(Once upon a Chassid).

SLEEP ENOUGH

A good night's sleep goes a long way towards a successful day. When a person is tired, problems feel insurmountable. When a person catches up on their sleep, they tend to feel that their problems are manageable. So it goes without saying that if you are tired then you deserve to go to bed early and get some extra rest. It is important to be there for others but to do that you must first be there for yourself.

RELAX AND REJUVENATE

Your emotional health is very important. You need time to relax and rejuvenate with a little tender loving care. The more you take care of your body, the better you can protect yourself from mood and hormone swings. Low periods are normal. Ideally, you want to treat them as if they are simple cases of "emotional flu". Lay low during these periods and avoid any serious interactions with others. Don't forget to exercise. It goes a long way towards improving your mood, clearing your mind, and melting your stress.

CULTIVATE OPTIMISM

HAPPINESS IS A STATE OF MIND

Happiness is not brought about by events, but by your state of mind. Ninety percent of your attitude towards life is due to how you view it, not what actually happens. Often there is a huge gap between your thoughts and your reality. You can have everything in the world and still be miserable. On the other hand, you can have relatively little and feel unbounded joy. The quality of your life is determined by the approach you choose. Essentially, your thoughts create the world you live in.

MAKE A CONSCIOUS CHOICE TO BE HAPPY

Many people dwell on their disappointments, instead of

thinking about their joyous achievements. Such people can manage to find reasons to be unhappy about a great school, or purposely seek a way to sabotage a meaningful friendship. Assume responsibility for making yourself happy. The ability to enjoy life is in your head. Surely it is wiser, and more desirable to say, "Life can be glorious!" than "Life is awful!" If you constantly anticipate pleasure, you can constantly be in a state of joy. Maybe that is why optimists live longer and healthier lives than pessimists.

Make a conscious choice to be happy – and work on it! Every moment can be filled with pleasure if you develop your awareness of this world's small treasures. Be conscious of Hashem's guiding Hand. If you make the effort to look for the positive aspects of your daily life, you will be pleasantly surprised. Much of what we do has so much hidden value. Every moment has the capability of bringing new happiness in its wake. Look for pursuits that offer profound, lasting satisfaction. The ripple effects of your good deeds have positive effects on you, your peers and your universe.

SEEK THE GIFTS IN EACH HURDLE YOU FACE

View your difficulties as hurdles to overcome and seek the gift, however small, in each hurdle you face. Being open to the possibility that your problems can teach you something is very empowering. Appreciate the small improvements in your day-to-day life.

Throughout the day, stop for a moment to recognize the fullness and joy of your life. Every time you truly feel pleasure, take note of it. Thank Hashem for what He has given you, and then carry that awareness back into your activities.

ROLE MODELS

Read about people who had difficult childhoods, over-came their impediments, and emerged as successful adults. Reading uplifting literature provides inspiration that can transform your life. When dealing with your own challeng-es, imagine how your role models would react. Imagine their confidence and act as they would.

> *When Rav Hillel Lichtenstein of Kolomaya was a child, he was bitten by a dog, which left him with a scar from the bite and a stutter from the trauma. The impedi-ment was so severe that his parents sent him to Nitra for therapy from a special teacher. After a few months there, the stutter disappeared.*
>
> *Later, as a teenager Reb Hillel contracted a severe lung ailment that left him so short of breath that he could not daven aloud but instead had to rely on thinking the tefillos. The doctors predicted the worst, but miraculous-ly, Reb Hillel recovered. Overcoming these obstacles, he became an outstanding lecturer. As an adult, he traveled around Eastern Europe strengthening the faith of the masses with his rousing speeches.*

AVOID THE DISCOURAGEMENT WHICH IS BEAMED YOUR WAY

Seek out great people who make you feel that it is pos-sible for you also to become great. Keep away from people who belittle your ambitions. A lot of discouragement is beamed your way on a regular basis. Encouraging you to be unhappy is a huge business. These companies want you to be insecure and unhappy and to believe that the only way you can be happy is to buy their product.

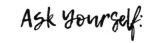

> **Ask Yourself:**
>
> **What internal and external factors are standing in the way of my happiness?**

SADNESS LOCKS THE
GATES OF HEAVEN.
PRAYER OPENS ALL LOCKED GATES.
JOY SHATTERS ALL BARRIERS

(BAAL SHEM TOV).

AVOID PROCRASTINATION

PROCRASTINATION SPOILS ONE'S CHANCES OF SUCCESS

You can plan and schedule, but if you do not take action, you will have no results. Procrastination is one of the most common causes of failure, spoiling one's chances of success. There is no shortage of excellent excuses for not doing something.

Procrastination can be caused by anything forced or imposed, the dreariness of the task, the need to change, the fear of the unknown or of a task that seems to be impossible or unpleasant, the fear of rejection or disapproval, or the fear of commitment or risk.

STRATEGIES TO AVOID PROCRASTINATION

Strategies that can help: break down a huge and overwhelming task to smaller "bite-size pieces". Think into the greater harm caused by evading or delaying an unpleasant task, then consider the gain to be had from action. Work on self-discipline and appreciate the opportunity to grow each time you overcome resistance to doing a necessary task. Tell others what you intend to do so you will feel forced to perform. Eliminate barriers and distractions. Reward yourself for accomplishment.

"THERE IS NO DANGER AS GREAT AS THE DANGER OF PROCRASTINATION"

(RAV MOSHE (HAIM LUZATTO).

COMMON CAUSES OF PROCRASTINATION

To overcome perfectionism - a common cause for procrastination - determine objectively how much time and effort should be spent collecting information and achieving results. I was once involved in a project that never got off the ground because the organizers would not proceed until every last detail was in place. Be responsible with all you undertake; always give your best effort. Warning: don't let a desire for perfectionism keep you from completing the task.

If you say I will do it but not right now, you are deceiving yourself. The truth is that you really do not wish to proceed either because of fear or because of laziness. If you are worried about something going wrong, make a "worst-case scenario list." Take a sheet of paper and draw a line down the middle. On the left side write down every possible catastrophe that you fear might happen. On the right side, mark down every disaster that actually does happen. Most people generally see that next to none of the calamities actually happen and they can afford to stop worrying - and stalling.

The over cautious person who takes no chances has to take whatever is left when others are through choosing. When you focus on problems, you will see more problems, when you focus on opportunities you will get more of them.

BEGIN NOW

Action breeds confidence and courage. Inaction breeds doubt and fear. The best antidote to fear and distress is to go out and get busy. Begin now with whatever tools you presently command. Better tools will appear as you proceed. Make your decisions carefully and deliberately but then, having made them put them to action as quickly as you can!

MULTITASKING

When the alarm clock rings, do you get up and begin the day or press the snooze button?

Do you offer to help your mother at home before reaching for the phone to shmooze with friends?

Idea: When you do want to shmooze, multitask – set the table, fold laundry, dust, clear away clutter, do the dishes.

You'll be surprised at how much you can accomplish, and you will train yourself well for the time when you will be running a home and will have very little time for just shmoozing. And what a treat for your parents!

Ask Yourself:

Do I make my *brachos* as soon as I finish eating or allow myself to get distracted?

Do I make sure to *daven* on time?

A group of community activists came to the Chazon Ish for advice. With his help, they resolved to undertake certain commitments. The Chazon Ish recognized that for all their good intentions, they were likely to procrastinate instead of putting their decisions into effect.

"It was Bilaam who advised the nobles of Moav to 'stay overnight,'" he reminded them. "Worthy decisions must be implemented immediately, and not be put off for tomorrow" (Zachor Le'David).

Rav Shmuel Markowitz passed Rav Shach and found him deep in thought. When Rav Shach noticed him, he said, "Do you know what I am thinking about now? I am thinking about what needs to be done tomorrow and considering if it is possible to do any of those things today" (Kinyan Torah).

EMBRACE ENTHUSIASM

ADVANTAGES OF ENTHUSIASM

Passion is a powerful spring. Its energy is a potent force. It allows you to put your whole soul into what you are doing. With confidence, you are a winner before you even get going. That is why most people's success is related to their enthusiasm. If you have an idea, or a problem or a wrong that you want to right and you are passionate about it, then with Hashem's help you will stick with it and succeed. "Ultimately there is more merit in the enthusiasm for the performance of a mitzvah then in fulfilling the commandment" (Rav Yerucham Levovitz).

Inspiration

The yetzer hara tries five ways to prevent a person from enthusiastically carrying out deeds.

He tells us:

- You have plenty of time
- It isn't far
- The journey is uncomplicated
- The reward is insignificant
- The Master will not mind if the job remains undone.

Rabi Tarfon dismisses all these five diversionary tactics when he says, "The day is short, the task is large, the laborers are lazy, the wage is great and the Master of the house is insistent" (Yaavetz).

ALWAYS DELIBERATE FIRST

Enthusiasm without deliberation can be dangerous. First, one must consider the best way to proceed and then take action (Malbim). Moving quickly is important so that one does not rest until he has completed the task to perfection (Ramchal). However, it should be like an ambulance driver hurrying to the hospital. Although it is true that he must hurry, he also has to be careful to avoid an accident (Rav BenZion Abba Shaul).

ENTHUSIASM IS CONTAGIOUS

It has been said that the only difference between try and triumph is a little umph. When you look back and see what you have accomplished the confidence will be vindicated. You can pull off anything if you are confident.

The person who has it in the right measure is generally a friend who is welcome. Enthusiasm is contagious. People respond well to enthusiastic individuals. They try to help them along.

MAKE WAVES

You don't want to just test the waters - you want to make waves. A person must be "bold as a leopard", to make a commitment to begin a project. He must also be "light as an eagle", and rise above any difficulties he encounters. An eagle is a heavy bird that relies on his powerful wings to soar above all threats. "Swift as a deer" sustaining the passion necessary to persist toward a goal and "strong as a lion" to complete a project (Rav Chaim Vital; Rav Shlomo Wolbe).

"A JEW SHOULD ALWAYS BE RUNNING. EITHER HE IS RUNNING TO PERFORM A MITZVAH OR RUNNING FROM A SIN"

(RAV YITZCHOK OF VORKE).

"'TAKING IT EASY' IS A TREIF TERM, SYMPTOMATIC OF AN UNHEALTHY APPROACH TO LIFE"

(RAV NOSSON WACHTFOGEL).

FAKE IT TILL YOU FEEL IT

"A tree in the darkness must be kicked until the light penetrates" (Zohar quoted by the Tanya). You must kick yourself if need be to force yourself to serve Hashem. Even if you don't feel enthusiastic about a mitzvah, behave as if you did and actively run to fulfill it. Sincere zeal will follow.

It is worth the effort because if a person has a fiery yearning to serve Hashem, he will never enter *Gehinnom*. Even were he to descend there, he would instantly be shot out like an arrow (*Shem Mi'Shmuel, Ki Sisa*).

 Food For Thought

The mayor of Bnei Brak, a Gerer chassid, once visited the Lubavitcher Rebbe. During the course of the conversation, he remarked to the Rebbe *men pruft ton vifil es iz meglech*—"we try to do as much as we're able".

The Rebbe looked at him in amazement, and exclaimed, *Meglech?! Dos iz al pi teva, vos far a shaychus hot a Yid mit teva*?!—"as much as possible i.e. naturally - what kind of a connection does a Jew have with nature?!"

A Jew has the ability to embrace the supernatural and accomplish amazing things.

The Chazon Ish once sent a family member on a mission to bring some money to a needy individual. When he saw that the relative did not leave immediately to

perform the task, he told him firmly, "A person must al-
ways react to such needs as if he has come face-to-face
with a blaze. One must move immediately."

When the beis midrash of the *Sefas Emes* burned
down the rebbe wanted to know the source of the fire. He
was told it was caused by a lit cigarette that was dropped
in the attic. The *Sefas Emes* exclaimed, "If a small fire can
create such a large conflagration, how much good can
come from a bit of the fire of Torah and mitzvos" *(Rav
Elimelech Biederman).*

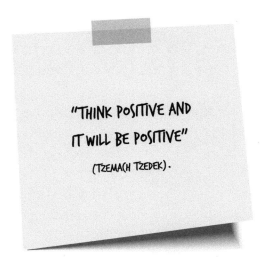

"THINK POSITIVE AND IT WILL BE POSITIVE"

(TZEMACH TZEDEK).

**There are certain emotions that the human psyche must
experience before the mind can accept them intellectually.**

*Harav Shraga Feivel Mendlowitz, zl, the legendary
menahel of Mesivta Torah Vodaas, was an individual
who did not simply perform or observe mitzvos; he lived
them. Carrying out a mitzvah was an experience that
penetrated his entire essence. Once, as a group of his students returned from Tashlich on Rosh Hashanah, Rav*

Shraga Feivel summoned them to come over. He was already sick at the time, nearing the end of his life.

He said to them, "After an entire day of davening, *I still do not feel that I have reached the level of* Malchiyos, *of declaring the total sovereignty of Hashem. Please help me. Perhaps together we might arouse ourselves to sense a taste of* Malchiyos." *He then began to sing slowly from the Rosh Hashanah davening:* V'yeida kol pa'ul ki Atah po'alto, *"Let everything that has been made know that You are the Creator", drawing the students into the* niggun, melody, *with him. They sang one* niggun *after another, and then Rav Shraga Feivel drew them into a dance to the words,* V'al kein nekaveh Lecha—"Therefore we put our trust in You". *They sang and danced with pure ecstasy.*

When they concluded, Rav Shraga Feivel thanked his students for helping him achieve his goal. The students also achieved a goal as tears of hisorerus - spiritual arousal, streamed down their faces. They had gone beyond reciting the words; they had embraced the emotional wellsprings of Hashem's sovereignty.

KEEP GROWING

DAILY CHESHBON HA'NEFESH

A daily *cheshbon ha'nefesh* plays an important role in our personal growth. Regular self-analysis will disclose whether you have advanced and if so how much. It will also reveal any backward steps one has taken. It helps you notice things that you are forgetting and helps you re-emphasize what you think is very important.

MAKING CHOICES

You are constantly making choices. Each decision, even a small one, brings with it new hope and promise. If you draw two lines and the second line veers slightly in another direction, if continued, it will result in the line moving in an entirely different direction.

View each choice as the beginning of a completely new path. This thought is extremely empowering and reassuring. At any point in time, you can change directions.

HOW TO TRANSFORM YOURSELF

A person can transform himself in one moment. You don't have to be someone special to make this type of change. Each one of you can revolutionize your behavior readily. Although it is difficult to abandon old habits, you must make up your mind that you will scrap the practices that hinder change, like a butterfly separating from its cocoon. You will do what is right in the eyes of Hashem. A little bit today and a little more tomorrow (Madreigas Ha'adam page 151).

> "A PERSON WHO DOESN'T STUDY WORKS OF SELF-IMPROVEMENT WILL BE CONSIDERED IN THE SAME CATEGORY AS SOMEONE WHO COMMITTED SUICIDE."
> RAV HILLEL OF KOLOMAYA

BEGIN NOW

Don't wait. Tomorrow you will wish that you had started today. Success takes time to build. Remember that there are no shortcuts anywhere worth going. The only person you should try to be better than is the person you were yesterday.

Ask Yourself:

What character traits do I want to make my own?

What kind of person do I want to be in two years from now? In five years?

These questions help you crystalize where you are going.

HIGHER THAN ANGELS

When we overcome our natural desires, transforming evil into good, we rise even higher than those who were born with naturally good traits, higher than angels, who have only perfect traits to begin with. "A person who toils to convert his darkness into light reaches the highest possible level" (Tiferes Shlomo, Terumah).

> When a chassid of the Tzemach Tzedek complained that his friends did not encourage him to improve spiritually the Tzemach Tzedek replied. "Demand it of yourself! Appeal to your conscience. Ask yourself, 'For what reason do I lack the desire to study Torah properly?' Why do I pray by rote, without proper feeling?'" (The Third Judge, page 32)

The Chovos Ha'levavos includes good character traits in

the list of things that promote good health (Shaar Ha'bitachon, Chapter 4). Because those who do not suffer from a bad temper or jealousy find their lives free of one of the number one killers: stress.

Everything you experience is a message from Hashem, calling us to come closer, and nothing is sweeter than receiving a personal message from our Father in Heaven.

"IF A MAN KNEW THAT THE 'EYES' OF G–D GO ALONGSIDE HIM AND SEE, HE WOULD NEVER SIN"

(VILNA GAON, SEFER DE'TZNIUSA 5IA).

PASSION AND PURPOSE

MOVE AHEAD WITH CONFIDENCE AND VIGOR

Many people go about their daily activities without thinking twice about what they are doing and why. They sit back passively waiting to see where life takes them next. When you see your path clearly marked, you can move ahead

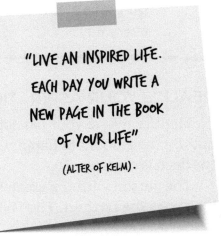

"LIVE AN INSPIRED LIFE. EACH DAY YOU WRITE A NEW PAGE IN THE BOOK OF YOUR LIFE"

(ALTER OF KELM).

with confidence and vigor. You can live actively and fully. A person without clear objectives becomes confused and dejected and simply exists.

IGNORE DISTRACTIONS

Successful students have a clear purpose when they walk into the classroom each day. They look for things they can learn and try to apply what they have mastered immediately. They focus closely on objectives and ignore distractions. They identify their biggest time wasters. A very knowledgeable seminary student once told me that on the way home she reviews the main points of the day's lessons.

Ask Yourself:

"Do I really need to spend two hours on the phone?"

Do I allow myself to be distracted by saying yes to everything and everyone?

Do I take small steps towards my goal every day?

REALIZE YOUR ASPIRATIONS

Identify where your passions lie. How do you figure that out? By the amount of happiness you are experiencing after the deed is completed.

The person with the greatest ambition is usually the one who goes the farthest. The *Ponovitcher* Rav was called "the

"YOUR MIND WILL ONLY ACT ON THOUGHTS THAT ARE MIXED WITH EMOTION"

(RAV YISROEL SALANTER).

"THE GREATNESS OF A MAN IS DIRECTLY PROPORTIONAL TO HIS SENSE OF RESPONSIBILITY"

(RABBI YERUCHAM LEVOVITZ).

dreamer" by his contemporaries. He forged ahead with determination and with Hashem's help, he realized many of his grand aspirations.

> When the foundation stone for Ponovitcher Yeshiva was put in place Rav Kahaneman declared, "Here will arise a yeshivah for six hundred boys. It will be the biggest yeshivah in the world."
>
> Those that were present smiled at the Ponovitcher Rav's unrealistic dream. The Holocaust had just come to an end. There was only a small amount of religious Jews in Eretz Yisroel and a tiny pool of potential yeshivah boys.
>
> Rav Yechezkel Avramsky commented, "You are dreaming." Rav Kahaneman didn't take it badly. He pleasantly replied, "Yes, yes, it is a dream, but I am not sleeping."

His dreams became a reality and the numbers continue to climb higher and higher.

AROUSE YOUR ENTHUSIASM

Practice saying to yourself, "Everyday, in every way, I am getting better and better." Arouse your enthusiasm by saying "When will I get a chance to fulfill this mitzvah? I will be so happy when this mitzvah comes my way."

Argue with the *yetzer hara*, "You will not dissuade me from serving Hashem." Imitate the tone of voice and expressions of those people you know who are good at getting things done. Try to follow their examples as best as you can.

CONSIDER THE REASON FOR YOUR ACTION

If you stop to think about the reason behind what you are doing you can boost your functioning and satisfaction. Even when you are schmoozing ask yourself, "Why am I doing this? What do I want to accomplish? The answer can be as simple as I want to enjoy myself and make a new friend or I want to let my friend know that I value our friendship. Being conscious of the outcome adds value to what you are doing. Knowing the exact results you want and acting with a clear purpose will instantly increase your chances of getting the outcome you want.

> *The Noda B'Yehudah was once asked if hunting was permissible. The questioner wondered if it might be forbidden to inflict pain on animals he did not intend to consume. The* Noda B'Yehudah *responded at length to the* halachic *question, but at the bottom of the response, he added a footnote: "I can't help but ask. How do you have time to hunt?"*

AVOID CONFLICT

Questions To Ask Yourself

To prevent conflict try asking yourself, "How does this person view the situation?" and, "What personal bias might be at the root of my position?" (Rabbi Z. Pliskin) These two questions reduce anger and resentment.

CHOOSE YOUR BATTLES

Be selective when choosing your battles. Rate the

difficulty on a scale of 1-10; tell yourself that you will not react to anything five or under. Opt to rate lower rather than higher. Try to forget about it or peacefully resolve the issue even if it means giving in. More serious issues that rate eight or nine and above, which have long term affects should be negotiated. People will take you more seriously when your negative responses are minimal. Also, you are better able to focus on your positions.

> "FOOLISHNESS FOLLOWS ANGER JUST AS CALMNESS REVEALS KNOWLEDGE AND A STRONG INTELLECT" (HA'MASPIK LE'OVDEI HASHEM).

> "YOU CANNOT MAKE PEOPLE DO WHAT WE WANT THEM TO DO, BUT WE CAN MAKE PEOPLE WANT TO DO WHAT WE WANT THEM TO DO" (RAV ELCHONON WASSERMAN).

COMMUNICATE RESPECTFULLY

If you have decided that the situation is worth getting angry about and there is something you can do to make it better, the key is to express your feelings in a considerate fashion. Anger, when communicated respectfully and channeled effectively, can be a tremendous source of energy and inspiration for change.

Offer a win-win solution. Seek a resolution where you

each get something you desire, and you will both walk away from the situation feeling happy and satisfied. Invest efforts into providing the other person with a way out (Rebbetzin Tziporah Heller).

Shortly before her petirah, someone got angry and screamed at Mrs. Henny Machlis in public, shaming her terribly. Mrs. Machlis, who was suffering tremendously from the progressive stages of her illness, remained calm and composed.

"Ima, how can you allow someone to talk to you that way?" her children asked.

"Can't you see she's hurting? Hurt people will hurt people," she replied, her voice full of sincere concern (Michal Trenk, Family First 22 Cheshvan 5776).

Shortly after Rav Chaim Epstein's passing, his family found a small paper in his wallet, enumerating items about which he felt a constant need to remind himself. Included among them were: "Strive for inner serenity and patience and be free of anger" and "Constantly consider what others are going through."

There was also a laminated card on his desk that read, pri habehalah charatah—*"the fruit of rage is regret".*

EVERYONE MAKES MISTAKES

SOMETIMES YOU SUCCEED AND OTHER TIMES YOU LEARN

It is well known that everybody makes mistakes. While some of us hesitate, others are busy making mistakes and becoming superior. Sometimes you succeed and other times you learn.

That's why they put erasers on pencils. Just reminding yourself that other people are also making mistakes (even in public) and that you are not the only one, can be a huge help. It can make you feel better about your choices and assure you that you are not alone.

ANALYZE YOUR MISTAKE BEFORE MOVING ON

A person who has never made a mistake has never tried anything new. Our mistakes are necessary to reach the places we have chosen to go. After you make a mistake and analyze it, you don't have to keep reminding yourself about it. You can forgive yourself and move on.

Accept the fact that mistakes are inevitable. If a person's behavior causes internal discomfort, this suggests that his soul is distressed by his current direction. When you make a mistake, don't jump to conclusions about your worth. What really is a reflection of your self-worth is how you treat mistakes. Are you able to gather your strength to make the necessary corrections, and allow yourself to bounce back? It becomes a real mistake if you learn nothing from the incident.

FORGIVE YOURSELF AND BEGIN ANEW

Even if a mistake is very costly or severe or big, that does not mean that you can't gain anything from it. When you make a really big mistake, and you are having a hard time dealing with it, talk to good friends or family about it. They may be able to offer you some kind words or advice to make you feel better. Most likely, they have made similar mistakes and can share their experiences. Always remember that *teshuvah* converts you into a changed person.

"WHEN A PERSON CRACKS OPEN AN EGG, HE DOES NOT HAVE TO EAT THE WHOLE THING TO DISCERN THAT IT IS ROTTEN"

(RAV SHLOMO OF RADOMSK).

Forget your past, forgive yourself and begin again, right now. The *yetzer hara* tries to bring you down by getting you to think about all the errors you have committed. Don't let him manipulate you.

MISTAKES TEACH YOU WHAT TO WORK ON

Without mistakes, how would you know what you have to work on? Experience helps you recognize a mistake when you make it again. When you knowingly repeat a mistake, it is no longer a mistake. It has become a decision.

> *Reb Simcha Bunim looked pale and out of sorts. When he was asked what was wrong, he replied, "Someone just pointed out my many failures to me."*
>
> *"How did you react?" asked the questioner.*
>
> *"I kissed him," Reb Simcha Bunim replied.*
>
> *He had actually been referring to the* mussar *work* Shevet Mussar. *Once he regained his composure, he kissed the volume in gratitude for enlightening him* (Simchas Yisroel, p. 29).

THE IMPORTANCE OF PERSISTENCE

SMALL EFFORTS CAN OFTEN RESULT IN GREAT REWARDS

In our generation, it is important to remind ourselves that we need only to make the effort to break through the barriers of our faults and limitations. Every effort readily ascends to Hashem because the paths have already been paved by our ancestors. The reward for even a small upward movement, and the nachas we're giving Hashem is infinite.

PERSISTENCE GETS THE BETTER OF FAILURE

It is vital that we don't give up. Perseverance requires that you focus on the result. One of the worst mistakes you can make is not completing something you have begun. Many of us are good starters but poor finishers. People tend to give up at the first signs of defeat. The person who embraces persistence discovers that failure becomes tired and departs. Failure cannot stand persistence. Persistence consistently gets the better of failure.

"A PERSON WHO IS NOT OVERWHELMED BY HIS PROBLEMS, BUT KNOWS HOW TO TAKE STOCK AND CONTINUE, WILL GET TO THE TOP OF THE MOUNTAIN" (REB YECHIEL MECHEL OF ZLOTCHOV).

FAIL TO QUIT

Perseverance is the quality that enables a person to overcome the inevitable obstacles and challenges that block his way. Forging ahead, over, or around those obstacles strengthens your ability to succeed. The ones who achieve their goals and realize their dreams are the ones that simply fail to quit. They persevere; they hang on, even when most of those around them have given up.

SMALL DAILY ACHIEVEMENTS ENERGIZE US

Serving Hashem is an ongoing commitment that never goes on vacation. Successful people keep moving. They review their goals and take *at least* one step towards achieving them *each day*. The key means to develop perseverance is consistently taking those small steps. Small achievements form a big success.

Think about solving a puzzle: you complete one section at a time until you eventually get the final image. If you take consistent, persistent action in the direction of your goals, you will achieve more than you ever imagined possible. The struggles, the little successes along the way, the recoveries from failures, help you develop a confidence that has actually been documented. Scientific studies have shown that these small daily achievements energize us, leaving us feeling good about ourselves.

When Rav Chaim Shmulevitz asked his uncle Rav Avrohom Yaffen who the best boy in his yeshivah was, he pointed not to the most brilliant or to the deepest of his students, but to Rav Yaakov Yisroel Kanievsky whose determination raised him above the others.

INCONVENIENCE OR CATASTROPHE?

AFFIRMATIVE INTERPRETATIONS

Generally, it is not what happens that causes our reaction but, rather, our interpretation of what happens. Most of our day is full of good things yet we tend to focus too much on the negative, allowing the isolated negative color our assessments. The equivalent would be looking at a beautiful painting and instead of appreciating the beauty, focusing on the fact that you don't like the signature.

NOTHING IS A CATASTROPHE

It is certainly normal for someone to become upset when facing life's challenges. Yet the Vilna Gaon categorizes the

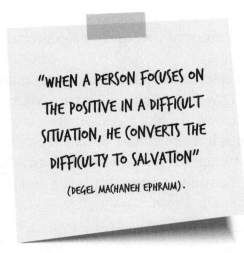

"WHEN A PERSON FOCUSES ON THE POSITIVE IN A DIFFICULT SITUATION, HE CONVERTS THE DIFFICULTY TO SALVATION"

(DEGEL MACHANEH EPHRAIM).

person who views an inconvenience as a catastrophe as a fool. The slings and arrows of outrageous people should elicit amusement, not irritation. "Don't be discouraged by the day-to-day difficulties, for they have no power over the person who increases his faith and strengthens his trust with a joyous heart" (Yesod Ha'AVodah). In other words, nothing is a catastrophe.

Practice finding a bright spot in our minor disappointments.

Ask Yourself:

"How can I view this situation in a different, more positive manner?"

EACH CHALLENGE HAS A CONSTRUCTIVE PURPOSE

When your friend leaves you waiting for an hour, your teacher gives you an undeserved lecture, your baby sister destroys your notes, you can easily point your finger. But why not rather remind yourself they are all Hashem's agents? Everything that happens to us has a reason. If not for the irritation caused by the grain of sand, oysters would never grow pearls.

Each challenge has a constructive purpose. Events could not have been different. This should be comforting. When you continually complain, you are like a person who is arrested and placed in chains. If he behaves calmly his chains hurt only a bit, but if he attempts to wriggle out of them and escape, the chains twist themselves about his body and he experiences a great deal of pain (Chofetz Chaim).

"IF A HORSE TURNS OFF THE PATH AND BEGINS TO GO ON ANOTHER, THE RIDER CAN SEIZE THE REINS AND REDIRECT IT ONTO THE PROPER PATH. IT IS THE SAME WITH THOUGHTS. AS SOON AS A PERSON SEES HIS THOUGHTS DEVIATING FROM THE PROPER PATH, HE MUST SEIZE THEM AND REDIRECT THEM TO THE PROPER WAY" (REBBE NACHMAN).

A Holocaust survivor who lived in Eretz Yisroel never stopped complaining. One day, he visited the Beis Yisroel of Ger for a blessing, but as was his wont, he began to grumble about his problems.

The Beis Yisroel stopped him and asked, "Do you have a way to make a living?"

"Yes," the man replied.

"Do you have a wife?" was the next question.

The answer was the same.

The Beis Yisroel then asked, "Do you have children and are they all healthy?"

The man again replied, "Yes."

"Then what do you have to complain about?" he roared, motioning for the man to leave.

When retelling the incident, the man declared, "The Rebbe was right. My life was saved, I married, I had healthy children and I earn a good living! What do I have to complain about?" (Asarah Nisyonos)

THE GRATITUDE ATTITUDE

MASTER THE ART OF APPRECIATING

Some people think that the only way to get more from Hashem is by complaining about all that they think they are missing. The truth is that when you are thankful for what you have and you express that gratitude openly, that's when Hashem provides even more. Take pride in your work and say thank You and Hashem will provide from His full and open Hand. The trick is to get into the habit of actively noticing. Once you master the art of observing, appreciating, and consciously enjoying what you have you will always be happy.

Notice your healthy body, your family members who

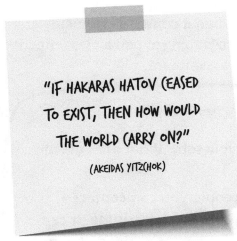

care about you, your friends, the roof over your head, the food on the table and the beautiful clothing you wear. Thank Hashem for pleasant news, for good conversation, for meeting someone admirable. Thank Hashem for the sunny day, the new experience, the good time with a friend. Feel good about overcoming a negative trait, dealing with conflict well and making someone else happy.

Each morning you thank Hashem for granting you everything you need to serve Him when you say the blessing, *"sheasah li kol tzarki"*. Pick gratitude exercises that work for you. Writing a list of all the good things you are grateful for, will impress the feelings of thankfulness on your consciousness. Do it repeatedly and feelings of gratitude will become habitual, built into your daily lives. Even if you find it difficult at first, rest assured that with practice you will blossom into an appreciative adult.

One size doesn't fit all when it comes to practicing gratitude and a gratitude practice is going to be a lot less effective if it is seen as a chore or an assignment.

Exercise

Repeatedly ask yourself, "What am I grateful for now?"

Think of three people you can contact right now to express your gratitude. It can be a parent, a neighbor, or a friend. It can be someone in your present life, or someone out of your past. Lift the phone and do it right away.

If you like a teacher let her know with a thank you letter or poem. Even a simple heartfelt letter means a lot to teachers. Try to find reasons to be grateful for the teachers you don't like.

GRATITUDE HELPS YOU GROW

Use gratitude to cultivate the growth mindset in difficult times. What did you learn from that terrible experience? What good came out of it,

"IF YOU FORGET HASHEM'S GOODNESS, YOU WILL EVENTUALLY FORGET HASHEM ENTIRELY" (OHR HA'CHAYIM).

despite the difficulty? The aim is to get to something along the lines of, "I am grateful that X happened, because otherwise I wouldn't have had Y opportunity!"

THE POWER OF *GAM ZU LE'TOVAH*

When *gam zu le'tovah* has been firmly imprinted in your mind, you will find that phrase at the ready whenever something occurs that seems to run counter to your expectations and wishes. You won't have to remember to bring that phrase to your mind. From deep within, the reminder that "this too is for the good" will pop up, and the situation you face will suddenly look different.

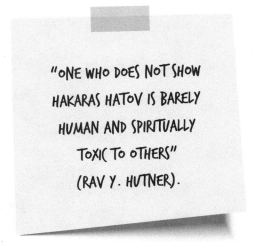

"ONE WHO DOES NOT SHOW HAKARAS HATOV IS BARELY HUMAN AND SPIRITUALLY TOXIC TO OTHERS" (RAV Y. HUTNER).

Once, when a student visited Rav Simcha Zissel Broide, the Rosh Yeshiva mentioned that he had come across a siddur that explained the tefillos based on Chazal. He had spent some time studying it, and was quite enthusiastic about what he had seen.

The student took the trouble to obtain a copy of the siddur and gave it to the Rosh Yeshivah as a present.

Not only did the Rosh Yeshivah thank him several times when he first presented the siddur, but five years later, Rav Simcha Zissel called him to thank him yet again. That morning, he had opened the siddur and read an explanation he greatly enjoyed, and he decided to call his student to tell him what a difference the siddur had made in his life (Prince of the Torah Kingdom).

HASHEM LOVES YOU

OUR BOND TO HASHEM CAN NOT BE SEVERED

The Jewish people have been chosen by Hashem for a close and intimate relationship. No-one will love you more or care for you more than Hashem. Our relationship with Hashem is unique in that it has both the aspect of parent-child relationship and the aspect of marriage. The former guarantees that this bond is unbreakable, since a child can never stop being the child of his or her parents. The latter shows that Hashem chose us for this relationship, fully aware of our strengths and weaknesses. The bond cannot be severed no matter how far away we stray from Hashem (Kiddushin 36a). Hashem's unconditional love for the Jewish people is a fundamental principle of Judaism (Rabbi Pinkus).

HASHEM IS OUR LOVING, DEVOTED FATHER

It's important for us to spend a little time every day remembering who we are - the descendants of Avrohom, Yitzchok and Yaakov, the children of righteous forbearers. Perhaps we may not always deserve Hashem's help but together with the merit of our ancestors, Hashem will surely help us.

Everything that happened to you from birth until this very moment has been sent your way by Hashem for your own good. When you recognize that everything you have is a gift, that leads to understanding that there is One who gives and is the source of all that is good: Hashem. Hashem is our loving, devoted Father. He knows exactly what you require and is constantly looking for opportunities to bestow good upon you. When you don't perceive how much Hashem loves you and how much He is giving you as an expression of that love, then you are voiding the purpose for which He created the world.

"A PERSON SHOULD ACCUSTOM HIMSELF TO REPEATING, 'ALL THAT HASHEM DOES IS FOR THE GOOD'" (SHULCHAN ARUCH).

It is the worst of evils to forget that one is a child of Hashem, and that Hashem's love for each Jew is incalculable. Hashem wants us to enjoy all the good He has provided.

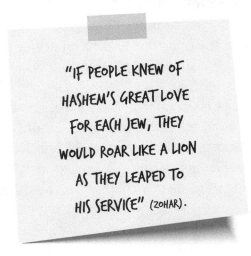

"IF PEOPLE KNEW OF HASHEM'S GREAT LOVE FOR EACH JEW, THEY WOULD ROAR LIKE A LION AS THEY LEAPED TO HIS SERVICE" (ZOHAR).

Close your eyes and feel Hashem's presence surrounding you. Try doing this again and again on a regular basis. See how relaxed you become when you really experience Hashem's presence.

When Rav Yitzchok Zev Yadler boarded a ship to Eretz Yisroel *with a young family, the other passengers stared at him in disbelief.*

"We are all old men who long to kiss the holy earth of Eretz Yisroel *before we die," said one man. "We have nothing to lose. But you are a young man with a family. How will you support them in a land where there is so much poverty?"*

"I'm not worried," replied Rav Yadler. "I have a wealthy father in Eretz Yisroel."

The passengers nodded in understanding. Some of

them even asked Rav Yitzchok Zev to speak to his father on their behalf, asking if he could help them as well when they arrived in Eretz Yisroel. Rav Yitzchok Zev smilingly assured them that his father was wonderfully kind, and would certainly be pleased to help them out.

When the boat finally arrived at the port, the passengers were surprised that no-one was there to greet Rav Yitzchok Zev.

"Where is your father?" they asked in concern.

"He is right here beside me, "he answered simply. "My father is the Father of us all, and He is fabulously wealthy. He has already welcomed us with open arms and He is the One to Whom we all turn for assistance" (U'reeh Be'tuv Yerushalayim).

Exercise

Recall an experience when you felt Hashem's helping Hand enabling you to put an end to a challenging situation.

BEING HONEST WITH OURSELVES

QUESTIONS TO ASK YOURSELF

Whatever your goal, whatever you want to do, determine why you are doing it and why it is important to you. It's hard to get anywhere if you don't know your internal motivating factors. Where are you now, which character traits brought you here? Equally important, ask yourself which mindsets are holding you back?

THE DELICATE BALANCE

Forging ahead sensibly is possible only when you know your good points and your bad points simultaneously (Rabbi Dr. A. J. Twerski). If I am only aware of my good points, I will likely view my success as the result of my efforts and fall prey to pride. If I see my faults and failures alone, I will become lazy and depressed. That is why the Rebbe Reb Bunim asked that a person work with two concepts, "You are but dust and ashes" and "the world was created for me". It is vital that one counter the other.

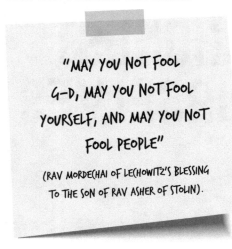

"MAY YOU NOT FOOL G-D, MAY YOU NOT FOOL YOURSELF, AND MAY YOU NOT FOOL PEOPLE"

(RAV MORDECHAI OF LECHOWITZ'S BLESSING TO THE SON OF RAV ASHER OF STOLIN).

THE ULTIMATE TRUTH

The most important character trait you must pursue is honesty. All faulty character traits spring from dishonesty. A person who dedicates himself to truth creates an angel that guides him along the path of righteousness (Tanna De'bei Eliyahu Zuta). Those who seek truth will merit seeing the Ultimate Truth. They will know and comprehend something of Hashem's Truth.

TRUTH IS POWERFUL LIGHT BEAM

Torah study develops a dedication to the ideals of truth and honesty. We have inherited a genetic predisposition to truth from Yaakov Avinu, the personification of truth. Rav Yehudah Segal recommended studying *mussar* to destroy the character flaws that deflect truth. A person who achieves an honest perspective can take control of his thoughts, speech and deeds. He will find himself emerging from darkness into

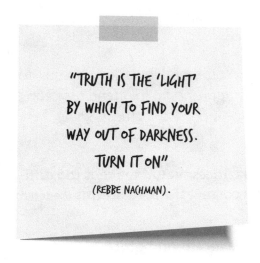

"TRUTH IS THE 'LIGHT'
BY WHICH TO FIND YOUR
WAY OUT OF DARKNESS.
TURN IT ON"

(REBBE NACHMAN).

light. Why go through life in the gloom of sightlessness? Rather acquire a truthful outlook, a powerful beam of light infusing life with meaningfulness and joy.

When Rabbi Dr. A.J. Twerski was asked how to prevent teens from getting involved in destructive/addictive behaviors, he explained that lying is the "oxygen" of addiction. Absolute truthfulness is the most powerful weapon a person has against addiction (Inyan, 3rd of Shevat 5776).

 The best way to master the art of being truthful is to...

- Be careful to tell the truth even with minor details

- Avoid even "white lies" or exaggerations

- Consider before speaking, especially when committing to doing something, so that you do not lie unintentionally

- Distance yourself from self-interest.

Two stories can explain the concept:

When Rav Isser Zalmen Meltzer was asked to write a letter of recommendation on someone's behalf, he would first write the letter and then decide whether or not he actually wished to pass it on.

When Rav Yosef Yoizel of Novardock needed to decide whether it was appropriate to attend a meeting in another city, he made a point of actually going there before deciding.

They were afraid that laziness would make it too difficult to determine what the correct thing to do was (Bederch Eitz Chaim).

- Think deeply into everything before speaking.
- Accept the advice of those who point out your personal deficiencies.
- Remember that lying to avoid unpleasant consequences will often lead to much more unpleasant consequences.
- If you realize belatedly that you did not tell the truth, force yourself to go back to the person you spoke to and correct yourself. When you make this a habit, you will automatically be more careful.

"MY DEAR CHILDREN, YOU NEED ONLY BE CAREFUL TO AVOID FALSEHOOD. THEN PERFECTION WILL BE WITHIN YOUR REACH AND THINGS WILL BE GOOD FOR YOU"

(BAAL SHEM TOV).

Five blind men encounter an elephant. One grabs the leg and is convinced that an elephant looks like a tree trunk. One seizes the tail and thinks that an elephant looks like a whip. Another touches the trunk and decides than an elephant looks like a hose. The fourth man pats the side and is sure that an elephant looks like a wall. The fifth grabs an ear, and believes that an elephant looks like a fan. The wise man tells them, "All of you are right and wrong."

What was their mistake? They reached conclusions without sufficient information. They should have shared their impressions with each other, putting all the pieces together until a clearer picture emerged. Each part of the truth must always be evaluated in the context of the whole.

APPENDIX

EXCERPT FROM A LETTER THAT RAV HUTNER WROTE TO ONE HIS STUDENTS:

When an ambitious young man of spirit and enthusiasm meets obstacles and falls, he imagines himself as unworthy of being "planted in the house of Hashem." He supposes that flourishing in the house of Hashem means to repose with calm spirit on "lush meadows" beside "tranquil waters" (*Tehillim* 23). He assumes that he should be able to delight in the *yetzer tov*, in the manner of the righteous "delighting in the reflection of the *Shechinah* in *Gan Eden*" and, at the same time, he should be untroubled by the agitation of the *yetzer hara*, along the lines of the verse, "Free among the dead" (*Tehillim* 88:6).

Know, however, my dear friend, that your soul is rooted not in the tranquility of the *yetzer tov*, but rather in the battle with the *yetzer hara*. And your precious, warm-hearted letter "testifies as one hundred witnesses" that you are a worthy warrior in the battalion of the *yetzer tov*. The English expression to "lose a battle and win a war" applies. Certainly, you have stumbled, and will stumble again (a self-fulfilling prophecy is not intended), and in many battles you will fall lame. I promise you, though, that after those losing campaigns, you will emerge from the war with laurels of victory upon your head and with fresh prey quivering between your teeth. Lose battles but win wars.

The wisest of all men has said, "a just man falls seven times and rises again" (*Mishlei* 24:16). Fools believe the intent of this verse is to teach us something remarkable - the just man has fallen seven times and yet he rises. But the knowledgeable are aware that the essence of the *tzaddik's* rising again is by way of his seven falls. "And He saw all that He had made and behold, it was very good." The "good" is the *yetzer tov* the "very good" is the *yetzer hara* (*Bereishis Rabbah* 91).

My cherished one, I clasp you to my heart, and whisper in your ear that had your letter reported on your *mitzvos* and good deeds, I would have said that I had received a good letter from you. As things stand, with your letter telling of slumps and falls and obstacles, I say that I have received a very good letter from you. Your spirit is storming as it aspires to greatness. I beg of you, do not portray for yourself great men as being as one with their *yetzer tov*. Picture, rather, their greatness in terms of an awesome war with every base and low inclination.

When you feel the turmoil of the *yetzer hara* within yourself, know that with that feeling, you resemble great men far more than with the feeling of deep peace which you desire. In those very areas where you feel yourself failing most frequently - particularly in those areas - you have the greatest potential for serving as an instrument of distinction for the honor of Hashem (Letters of *Pachad Yitzchok* 128).

ABOUT THE AUTHOR

Reb. S. Feldbrand is an educator and writer. For decades, she has been engaged in *kiruv*, while also teaching high school and seminary. She has had a remarkable career as a principal of Ohel Sorah Seminary (Montreal), Moreshes Seminary (Lakewood), Bnos Chava High School (Brooklyn), and Elyon Seminary (Brooklyn).

Rebbetzin Feldbrand has written over twenty books thus far. Her bestselling works include both fiction and non-fiction (see "Books by the Same Author" on the back cover). Some of her books have been translated into French, German and Russian.

Rebbetzin Feldbrand is currently available to conduct workshops on topics such as *tefillah* and personal growth.

She also counsels, mainly through her e-mail address: ask.
the.rebetzin@gmail.com.

Rebbetzin Feldbrand has two manuscripts in the works.
For sponsorship opportunities, please contact info@israel-
bookshoppublications.com.